W9-AEB-807

Praise for *Peter Drucker's Five Most Important Questions*

"As a marketer and a business leader I have found guidance in Drucker's simple wisdom. My favorite: 'Without a customer, there is no business.' This book offers timeless insights, an anecdote for those dizzied by the rapidly evolving business landscape."

— *Beth Comstock, Chief Marketing Officer, GE*

"A timeless guide for students at the Yale School of Management— elegant in its simplicity yet powerful in focus."

— *General Thomas Kolditz, Professor and Director, Leadership Development Program, Yale School of Management*

"Nobody, not even Socrates, has ever asked better questions than Peter Drucker. All the personality, all the wisdom is here to make your work dramatically more effective. There's nothing better. It's like having Peter at your side."

— *Bob Buford, Author,* Halftime *and* Finishing Well, *and Founding Chairman, Peter F. Drucker Foundation for Nonprofit Management*

"In my work with chief executives, managers, and students, I see a shared desire to create a life of meaning, purpose and passion. This book shares essential lessons to do so for all generations. Memorable, powerful, and accessible, this is another classic in the making!"

— *Sanyin Siang, Executive Director, Fuqua/Coach K Center on Leadership & Ethics (COLE), Duke University*

PETER DRUCKER'S

FIVE MOST IMPORTANT QUESTIONS

ENDURING WISDOM FOR YOUNG LEADERS

PETER F. DRUCKER

WITH FRANCES HESSELBEIN, JOAN SNYDER KUHL, BERNARD BANKS, LAUREN MAILLIAN BIAS, JUANA BORDAS, ADAM BRAUN, JIM COLLINS, CAROLINE GHOSN, KELLY GOLDSMITH, MARSHALL GOLDSMITH, NADIRA HIRA, PHILIP KOTLER, JIM KOUZES, RAGHU KRISHNAMOORTHY, KASS LAZEROW, MIKE LAZEROW, LUKE OWINGS, MICHAEL RADPARVAR, V. KASTURI RANGAN, AND JUDITH RODIN

EDITED BY PETER ECONOMY

WILEY

Published by John Wiley & Sons, Inc., Hoboken, New Jersey.
Published simultaneously in Canada.

For general information about our other products and services, please contact our Customer Care Department within the United States at (800) 762-2974, outside the United States at (317) 572-3993 or fax (317) 572-4002.

Wiley publishes in a variety of print and electronic formats and by print-on-demand. Some material included with standard print versions of this book may not be included in e-books or in print-on-demand. If this book refers to media such as a CD or DVD that is not included in the version you purchased, you may download this material at http://booksupport.wiley.com. For more information about Wiley products, visit www.wiley.com.

ISBN 978-1-118-97959-4 (cloth); ISBN 978-1-118-97961-7 (ebk);
ISBN 978-1-118-97960-0 (ebk)

Printed in the United States of America

10 9 8 7 6 5 4 3 2 1

CONTENTS

FOREWORD

In 2000, Fred Andrews wrote in *The New York Times* of the Peter F. Drucker Foundation for Nonprofit Management—now The Frances Hesselbein Leadership Institute: "With little money, the Institute is a pool of management wisdom for all who choose to dip their cup." Today, we celebrate the Institute's 25th anniversary. Our work has not deviated far from our work in 1990, or 2000: we continue to publish the most contemporary writing on leadership and management; we provide relevant leadership resources, advice and inspiration; we introduce cross-sector partnerships that provide opportunities for learning and growth; and we support student-leaders and professionals around the globe.

I'm encouraged by the "Bright Future" message of leaders across the sectors who are using *The Five Questions*—who are reaching into their organization and out to their customers and community, reaffirming their values, and reexamining their mission.

Since we first published *The Five Questions,* I've met many "fellow travelers"—working professionals, high-level executives, cadets, faculty, students—who tell us that the inspiration and leadership resources we offer, rooted in the leadership work of Peter F. Drucker, has allowed them to embody more fully our *To Serve Is To Live* leadership philosophy, as well as share our mission-focused, values-based leadership model with others in their wider community. These leaders have realized that simple questions are sometimes the hardest to answer. Peter Drucker's questions are profound, and answering them requires us to make stark and honest self-assessments.

If Peter were with you and your organization today, we believe he would ask the same five questions he developed when our journey of self-assessment began with him:[1]

1. What is our mission?
2. Who is our customer?
3. What does the customer value?
4. What are our results?
5. What is our plan?

Complex and compelling—these questions are essential and relevant. They can be applied to any organization today. This book is designed for *organizational,* strategic self-assessment, not for *program* assessment or for an *individual* performance review. It starts with the fundamental question, "What is our mission?" It addresses the question of the organization's reason for being—its purpose—not the *how.* The mission inspires; it is what you want your organization to be remembered for. The questions then guide you through the process of assessing *how well you are doing,* ending with a measurable, results-focused strategic plan to further the mission and to achieve the organization's goals, guided by the vision.

The ultimate beneficiaries of this very simple process are the people or customers touched by your organization and by others, like you, who have made the courageous decision to look within yourselves and your organization, identify strengths and challenges, embrace change, foster innovation, accept and respond to customer feedback, look beyond the organization for trends and opportunities, encourage planned abandonment, and demand measurable results. Some organizations of the past rested on good deeds alone. Organizations of the future are relevant and sustainable with measurable results.

This self-assessment model is flexible and adaptable. Walk this tool into any boardroom or CEO's office. Use it in any sector—public, private, or social. It does not matter whether the organization is a Fortune 500 multinational or a small entrepreneurial start-up, a large national government agency or one that serves your local town or regional heartland, or a billion-dollar nonprofit foundation or a $100,000 homeless shelter. What matters is commitment to the mission, commitment to the customer, commitment to the future, and commitment to innovation. Self-discovery is an introspective and courageous journey that gives organizations and leaders the energy and courage to grow.

In this enhanced edition of the indispensable tool, we have considered the context of our times, the advent of the B Corporation, which allows organizations to account for the commitments they are making to their customers, their employees, the environment, and the community at large, the impact we are seeing from the Millennial generation—a generation for whom *To Serve Is To Live* is not a foreign language. We have convened emerging and experienced leaders of the future who offer us new insight to these powerful five questions.

We are deeply grateful for the generous gift of our respected and admired contributors:

- Col. Bernard Banks, who explores the importance of examining an organization's results through the prism of organizational and personal values.
- Lauren Maillian Bias, who describes the interdependence of personal success and professional success.
- Juana Bordas, who considers how best to measure the effectiveness of an organization's planning process and how those who want to start their own ventures can apply the lessons she learned from successfully starting up Colorado's largest Hispanic-serving organization.
- Adam Braun, who explores the nature of achieving one's goals and how the finish line to living the perfect life does not exist.
- Jim Collins, who describes how an organization's strategy reflects the fundamental tension between continuity and change and how organizations excellent at adapting to change know what should *not* change.
- Caroline Ghosn, who states that the most important thing you can do as a leader is to articulate a vision and that translating the vision into action requires a clear plan—something tangible that people can make their own.

- Marshall and Kelly Goldsmith, who explore the personal application of the question, "What is our mission?" and have found through their research that creating an effective personal mission requires taking into account both happiness *and* meaning.

- Nadira Hira, who suggests that more than ever before, companies today have access to a constant stream of feedback in the form of social media but that too few know how to use it effectively.

- Philip Kotler, who implores us to better understand who our key customers are and plan to please them instead of trying to please everyone in an unfocused way.

- Jim Kouzes, who suggests that everything exemplary leaders do is about creating value for their customers.

- Raghu Krishnamoorthy, who explains how General Electric constantly reimagines and reinvents itself to respond to shifting customer needs and to remain relevant in today's fast-changing global markets.

- Joan Snyder Kuhl, who describes who the Millennials are, what they want and how Drucker's enduring wisdom is as relevant to them today as it was for their predecessors.

- Mike and Kass Lazerow, who announce the arrival of the customer revolution—a radical shift of power from companies to their connected customers—and how companies, and the people who lead them, can and must jump onboard.

- Luke Owings, who cautions readers not to ignore the needs of supporting customers and explains how the ability to recognize their needs and motivations can propel the organization's mission forward.

- Michael Radparvar, who tells the story about the origins of the popular Holstee manifesto and how this manifesto transformed into the company's own mission statement.

- V. Kasturi Rangan, who describes what makes a good plan and the importance of monitoring plan execution and closing the feedback loop for the next planning cycle.

- Judith Rodin, who asserts that no plan can be considered complete—or satisfactory—until it produces measurable outcomes and incorporates mechanisms that allow midcourse corrections based on results.

Their thoughtful perspectives will inspire you, and we know you will be as appreciative of their generous gifts of wisdom, experience, and intellectual energy as we are. The original *The Five Most Important Questions* emerged from the wisdom of Drucker. We once again share Drucker's wisdom, this time enriched with the thoughts of new great leaders. We are deeply grateful to you, our readers and supporters, fellow travelers on the journey to organizational self-discovery.

FRANCES HESSELBEIN
Founding President, President and CEO
Frances Hesselbein Leadership Institute
New York City

INTRODUCTION

CREATING ENDURING WISDOM FOR TODAY'S LEADERS

Peter F. Drucker often asked those he worked with a simple question: "What do you want to be remembered for?"

At the Frances Hesselbein Leadership Institute, we unanimously agree that it's vitally important that we play a role in inspiring the next generation of leaders. In 2009, the Hesselbein Institute partnered with the University of Pittsburgh to launch the Hesselbein Global Academy for Student Leadership and Civic Engagement, which has already convened 300 talented students from every continent and exposed them to Peter F. Drucker's and Frances Hesselbein's work.

Today's youngest generation—known as the Millennials or Generation Y, born between 1980 and 2000—are not only the largest generation yet but also the most educated and most diverse. The reach of technology and ease of global travel have magnified the creativity of their dreams in many ways. The digital and social media movement from traditional cable to Facebook and Twitter put them in touch with the rest of the world where they can wear, consume, and interact with global brands and causes in new and unprecedented ways. They developed networks of friends who were not neighbors or in their gym class but from faraway parts of the world. They may never meet these friends face to face, yet the connections are highly influential upon their lives. They have developed a global sensibility, which is why I often refer to Millennials as the *first global* generation.

The young leaders we meet are driven, generous, and globally minded self-starters. They see the world differently, with a relentlessly positive attitude. At the same time, they are facing record unemployment and underemployment, and they feel very misunderstood in the workplace and media.

What we have learned is that Millennials are craving guidance, simple tools, and mentors to help them focus, achieve their potential, and pursue their dreams of making a difference in the world. Which brings us to this book. Is Drucker's management philosophy still relevant to today's young talent and tenured leadership? Yes! Can it make a difference? We've seen it happen. It's hard to believe that words written in the mid-twentieth century might still be applicable to today's business challenges and opportunities, but we provide examples throughout the book to prove just that.

Drucker says that "self-assessment is the first action required of leadership," so it makes sense that the five questions tool is read by young talent who are on the path to one day leading organizations, and re-read by experienced leaders in diverse sectors. This basic framework has served leaders in every sector for decades and is the perfect companion for Millennials and management today. Our contributors shine a light on several examples of how the self-assessment process can serve any purpose and stimulate progress.

The war for global talent is in full swing. Executives and organizations in every sector are looking for strategies to amplify the productivity of their younger workforce and grow their skills toward sustainable leadership. Our hope in launching this new edition is to build awareness and cultivate a new community of Drucker fans who will communicate using this basic language of The Five Questions. This can also be a foundational tool for new-manager and leadership-development programs. Drucker's thought leadership can serve as a universal, collaborative platform for developing ideas and strategic plans within a multigeneration team in any environment and sector. Just the act of reflecting on Drucker's influential insights can promote the kind of dialogue that will bring your team closer together and bridge the common communication gap between the different generations.

Millennials are committed to the success of the social sector, and we have found college students are volunteering all over the globe. In one of my national research studies of college students, 70.0 percent of freshmen and 79.1 percent of juniors and seniors reported volunteering while in college.[1] The Millennial generation will continue to seek opportunities to connect the mission of nonprofit organizations to for-profit partners. Great leaders "think of the needs and the opportunities of the organization," Drucker wrote, "before they think of their own needs and opportunities."

As a mentor to undergraduate and master of business administration (MBA) students, I've observed a dramatic shift in their expectations and anxieties regarding postcollege career opportunities. The financial crisis led many companies to change their workforce dramatically, which deflated the sense of security most employees associate with the larger companies. MBA graduates today are becoming more selective in their postgraduate pursuits and setting their sights on new ventures that allow them more responsibility and where they perceive they will gain a deeper understanding of the enterprise. Business schools are encouraging the swelling interest in start-ups through business plan competitions and new media and venture-related courses.

More Millennials are starting businesses than any previous generation, fleeing cubicles in corporate America to launch their passion projects. According to Bloomberg, 8 out of 10 entrepreneurs who start businesses fail within the first 18 months. In many cases, failure is because of lack of focus in the business strategy, along with a lack of funding. To garner investment and support from others, you must demonstrate core knowledge and laser focus for your business. What better way to build your business than to use the five questions self-assessment tool as your foundation?

Frances Hesselbein is a descendant of the second president of the United States, John Adams, who said, "If your actions inspire others to dream more, learn more, do more, and become more, you are a leader." We are in deep gratitude to the leaders who connected their insights to Drucker's enduring wisdom throughout this book to inspire and unleash the potential of the Millennial generation!

JOAN SNYDER KUHL
Founder, Why Millennials Matter
Member, Board of Governors
Frances Hesselbein Leadership Institute
New York City

ABOUT PETER F. DRUCKER

Peter F. Drucker (1909–2005)—widely considered the world's foremost pioneer of management theory—was a writer, teacher, and consultant specializing in strategy and policy for businesses and social sector organizations. Drucker's career as a writer, consultant, and teacher spanned nearly 75 years, and he worked with a wide variety of organizations, including Procter & Gamble, General Electric, IBM, Girl Scouts of the USA, the Red Cross, and others. His groundbreaking work turned modern management theory into a serious discipline. He has influenced or created nearly every facet of its application, including decentralization, privatization, empowerment, and understanding of the knowledge worker. He authored 39 books and numerous scholarly and popular articles. He was an editorial columnist for the *Wall Street Journal* and a frequent contributor to the *Harvard Business Review* and other periodicals.

Drucker was born in 1909 in Vienna and was educated there and in England. He earned his doctorate in public and international law while working as a newspaper reporter in Frankfurt, Germany. He then worked as an economist for an international bank in London. Drucker moved to London in 1933 to escape Hitler's Germany and took a job as a securities analyst for an insurance firm. Four years later, he married Doris Schmitz, and the couple departed for the United States in 1937.

Drucker landed a part-time teaching position at Sarah Lawrence College in New York in 1939. He joined the faculty of Bennington College in Vermont as professor of politics and philosophy in 1942 and the next year put his academic career on hold to spend two years studying the management structure of General Motors. This experience led to his book *Concept of the Corporation,* an immediate best seller in the United States and Japan, which validated the notion that great companies could stand among humankind's noblest inventions. For more than 20 years, he was professor of management at the graduate business school of New York University. He was awarded the Presidential Citation, the university's highest honor.

Drucker moved to California in 1971, where he was instrumental in the development of the country's first executive master of business administration program for working professionals at Claremont Graduate University (then known as Claremont Graduate School). The university's management school was named the Peter F. Drucker Graduate School of Management in his honor in 1987. He taught his last class at the school in the spring of 2002.

His courses consistently attracted the largest number of students of any class the university offered.

As a consultant, Drucker specialized in strategy and policy for governments, businesses, and nonprofit organizations. His special focus was on the organization and work of top management. He worked with some of the world's largest businesses and with small and entrepreneurial companies. In his later years, Drucker worked extensively with nonprofit organizations, including universities, hospitals, and churches. He served as a consultant to a number of agencies of the U.S. government and with the governments of Canada, Japan, Mexico, and other nations throughout the world.

Drucker has been hailed in the United States and abroad as the seminal thinker, writer, and lecturer on the contemporary organization. Drucker's work has had a major influence on modern organizations and their management for more than 60 years. Valued for keen insight and the ability to convey his ideas in popular language, Drucker often set the agenda in management thinking. Central to his philosophy is the view that people are an organization's most valuable resource and that a manager's job is to prepare and free people to perform. In 1997, he was featured on the cover of *Forbes* magazine under the headline "Still the Youngest Mind," and *Businessweek* has called him "the most enduring management thinker of our time."

On June 21, 2002, Drucker, author of *The Effective Executive* and *Management Challenges for the 21st Century*, received the Presidential Medal of Freedom—the nation's highest civilian honor—from President George W. Bush.

Drucker received honorary doctorates from numerous universities around the world, including universities in the United States, Belgium, Czechoslovakia, Great Britain, Japan, Spain, and Switzerland. He was the founding chairman of the Peter F. Drucker Foundation for Nonprofit Management, now the Frances Hesselbein Leadership Institute. He passed away on November 11, 2005, at age 95.

WHY
SELF-ASSESSMENT?

Peter F. Drucker

The ninety million volunteers who work for nonprofit institutions—America's largest employer—exemplify the American commitment to responsible citizenship in the community. Indeed, nonprofit organizations are central to the quality of life in America and are its most distinguishing feature.

Forty years ago management was a very bad word in nonprofit organizations. Management meant *business*, and the one thing a nonprofit was not was a *business*. Today, nonprofits understand that they need management all the more because they have no conventional bottom line. Now they need to learn how to use management so they can concentrate on their mission. Yet, there are few tools available that address the distinct characteristics and central needs of the many nonprofit organizations in America.

Although I don't know a single for-profit business that is as well managed as a few of the nonprofits, the great majority of the nonprofits can be graded a "C" at best. Not for lack of effort; most of them work very hard. But for lack of *focus*, and for lack of *tool competence*. I predict that this will change, however, and we at the Drucker Foundation [now the Frances Hesselbein Leadership Institute] hope to make our greatest impact in these areas of focus and tool competence.

For years, most nonprofits felt that good intentions were by themselves enough. But today, we know that because we don't have a bottom line, we have to manage *better* than for-profit business. We have to have discipline rooted in our mission. We have to manage our limited resources of people and money for maximum effectiveness. And we have to think through very clearly what results are for our organization.[1]

THE FIVE MOST IMPORTANT QUESTIONS

The self-assessment process is a method for assessing what you are doing, why you are doing it, and what you *must* do to improve an organization's performance. It asks the five essential questions: *What is our mission? Who is our customer? What does the customer value? What are our results?* and *What is our plan?* Self-assessment leads to action and lacks meaning without it. To meet growing needs and succeed in a turbulent and exacting environment, social sector organizations must focus on mission, demonstrate accountability, and achieve results.[2]

The self-assessment tool forces an organization to focus on its mission. About eight out of ten nonprofits in the country are small organizations whose leaders find it very hard to say no when someone comes to them with a good cause. I advised some close friends of mine, working with a local council of churches, that half the things they are doing they shouldn't be doing—not because they're unimportant but because they're not needed. I told them, "Other people can do those activities and do them well. Maybe a few years ago it was a good idea for you to help get this farmers' market started because those Vietnamese farmers in your area needed a place to sell their produce; but it's going well now, and you don't have to run it anymore. It's time for organized abandonment."[3]

You cannot arrive at the right definition of results without significant input from your *customers*—and please do not get into a debate over that term. In business, a customer is someone you must satisfy. If you don't, you have no results. And pretty soon you have no business. In a nonprofit organization, whether you call the customer a student, patient, member, participant, volunteer, donor, or anything else, the focus must be on what these individuals and groups value—on satisfying their needs, wants, and aspirations.

The danger is in acting on what *you* believe satisfies the customer. You will inevitably make wrong assumptions. Leadership should not even try to guess at the answers; it should always go to customers in a systematic quest for those answers. And so, in the self-assessment process, you will have a three-way conversation with your board, staff, and customers and include each of these perspectives in your discussions and decisions.[4]

PLANNING IS NOT AN EVENT

When you follow the self-assessment process through to its completion, you will have formulated a plan. Planning is frequently misunderstood as making future decisions, but decisions exist only in the present. You must have overarching goals that add up to a vision for the future, but the immediate question that faces the organization is not what to do tomorrow. The question is, What must we do *today* to achieve results? Planning is not an event. It is the continuous process of strengthening what works and abandoning what does not, of making risk-taking decisions with the greatest knowledge of their potential effect, of setting objectives, appraising performance and results through systematic feedback, and making ongoing adjustments as conditions change.[5]

ENCOURAGE CONSTRUCTIVE DISSENT

All the first-rate decision makers I've observed had a very simple rule: If you have quick consensus on an important matter, don't make the decision. Acclamation means nobody has done the homework. The organization's decisions are important and risky, and they *should* be controversial. There is a very old saying—it goes all the way to Aristotle and later became an axiom of the early Christian Church: In essentials unity, in action freedom, and in all things trust. Trust requires that dissent come out in the open.[6]

Nonprofit institutions need a healthy atmosphere for dissent if they wish to foster innovation and commitment. Nonprofits must encourage honest and constructive disagreement precisely because everybody is committed to a good cause: Your opinion versus mine can easily be taken as your good faith versus mine. Without proper encouragement, people have a tendency to avoid such difficult, but vital, discussions or turn them into underground feuds.

Another reason to encourage dissent is that any organization needs its nonconformist. This is not the kind of person who says, "There is a right way and a wrong way—and our way." Rather, he or she asks, "What is the right way *for the future?*" and is ready to change. Finally, open discussion uncovers what the objections are. With genuine participation, a decision doesn't need to be sold. Suggestions can be incorporated, objections addressed, and the decision itself becomes a commitment to action.[7]

CREATING TOMORROW'S SOCIETY OF CITIZENS

Your commitment to self-assessment is a commitment to developing yourself and your organization as a leader. You will expand your vision by listening to your customers, by encouraging constructive dissent, by looking at the sweeping transformation taking place in society. You have vital judgments ahead: whether to change the mission, whether to abandon programs that have outlived their usefulness and concentrate resources elsewhere, how to match opportunities with your competence and commitment, *how you will build community and change lives.* Self-assessment is the first action requirement of leadership: the constant resharpening, constant refocusing, never being really satisfied. And the time to do this is when you are successful. If you wait until things start to go down, then it's very difficult.

We are creating tomorrow's society of citizens through the social sector, through *your* nonprofit organization. And in that society, everybody is a leader, everybody is responsible, everybody acts. Therefore, mission and leadership are not just things to read about, to listen to; they are things to *do* something about. Self-assessment can and should convert good intentions and knowledge into effective action—not next year but tomorrow morning.[8]

WHAT IS OUR MISSION?

Peter F. Drucker

- What is the current mission?
- What are our challenges?
- What are our opportunities?
- Does the mission need to be revisited?

———

Each social sector institution exists to make a distinctive difference in the lives of individuals and in society. Making this difference is the mission—the organization's purpose and very reason for being. Each of more than one million nonprofit organizations in the United States may have a very different mission, but *changing lives* is always the starting point and ending point. A mission cannot be impersonal; it has to have deep meaning, be something you believe in—something you know is right. A fundamental responsibility of leadership is to make sure that everybody knows the mission, understands it, lives it.

Many years ago, I sat down with the administrators of a major hospital to think through the mission of the emergency room. As do most hospital administrators, they began by saying, "Our mission is health care." And that's the wrong definition. The hospital does not take care of health; the hospital takes care of illness. It took us a long time to come up with the very simple and (most people thought) too-obvious statement that the emergency room was there *to give assurance to the afflicted.* To do that well, you had to know what really went on. And, to the surprise of the physicians and nurses, the function of a good emergency room in their community was to tell eight out of ten people there was nothing wrong that a good night's sleep wouldn't fix. "You've been shaken up. Or the baby has the flu. All right, it's got convulsions, but there is nothing seriously wrong with the child." The doctors and nurses gave assurance.

We worked it out, but it sounded awfully obvious. Yet translating the mission into action meant that everybody who came in was seen by a qualified person in less than a minute. The first objective was to see everybody, almost immediately—because that is the only way to give assurance.

IT SHOULD FIT ON A T-SHIRT

The effective mission statement is short and sharply focused. It should fit on a T-shirt. The mission says *why* you do what you do, not the means by which you do it. The mission is broad, even eternal, yet directs you to do the right things now and into the future so that everyone in the organization can say, "What I am doing contributes to the goal." So it must be clear, and it must inspire. Every board member, volunteer, and staff person should be able to see the mission and say, "Yes. This is something I want to be remembered for."

To have an effective mission, you have to work out an exacting match of your opportunities, competence, and commitment. Every good mission statement reflects all three. You look first at the outside environment. The organization that starts from the inside and then tries to find places to put its resources is going to fritter itself away. Above all, it will focus on yesterday. Demographics change. Needs change. You must search out the accomplished facts—things that have already happened—that present challenges and opportunities for the organization. Leadership has no choice but to anticipate the future and attempt to mold it, bearing in mind that whoever is content to rise with the tide will also fall with it. It is not given to mortals to do any of these things well, but, lacking divine guidance, you must still assess where your opportunity lies.

Look at the state of the art, at changing conditions, at competition, the funding environment, at gaps to be filled. The hospital isn't going to sell shoes, and it's not going into education on a big scale. It's going to take care of the sick. But the specific aim may change. Things that are of primary importance now may become secondary or totally irrelevant very soon. With the limited resources you have—and I don't just mean people and money but also competence—where can you dig in and make a difference? Where can you set a new standard of performance? What really inspires your commitment?

MAKE PRINCIPLED DECISIONS

One cautionary note: *Never subordinate the mission in order to get money.* If there are opportunities that threaten the integrity of the organization, you must say no. Otherwise, you sell your soul. I sat in on a discussion at a museum that had been offered a donation of important art on conditions that no self-respecting museum could possibly accept. Yet a few board members said, "Let's take the donation. We can change the conditions down the road." "No, that's unconscionable!" others responded, and the board fought over the issue. They finally agreed they would lose too much by compromising basic principles to please a donor. The board forfeited some very nice pieces of sculpture, but core values had to come first.

KEEP THINKING IT THROUGH

Keep the central question What is our mission? in front of you throughout the self-assessment process. Step by step you will analyze challenges and opportunities, identify your customers, learn what they value, and define your results. When it is time to develop the plan, you will take all that you have learned and revisit the mission to affirm or change it.

As you begin, consider this wonderful sentence from a sermon of that great poet and religious philosopher of the seventeenth century, John Donne: "Never start with tomorrow to reach eternity. Eternity is not being reached by small steps." We start with the long range and then feed back and say, "What do we do *today?*" The ultimate test is not the beauty of the mission statement. The ultimate test is your performance.[1]

WHAT IS OUR MISSION?

Jim Collins

What is our mission? Such a simple question—but it goes right to the heart of the fundamental tension in any great institution: the dynamic interplay between continuity and change. Every truly great organization demonstrates the characteristic of *preserve the core, yet stimulate progress.* On the one hand, it is guided by a set of core values and fundamental purpose—a core mission that changes little or not at all over time; and, on the other hand, it stimulates progress: change, improvement, innovation, renewal. The core mission remains fixed while operating practices, cultural norms, strategies, tactics, processes, structures, and methods continually change in response to changing realities. Indeed, the great paradox of change is that the organizations that best adapt to a changing world first and foremost know what should *not* change; they have a fixed anchor of guiding principles around which they can more easily change everything else. They know the difference between what is truly sacred and what is not, between what should never change and what should be always open for change, between "what we stand for" and "how we do things."

The best universities understand, for example, that the ideal of freedom of inquiry must remain intact as a guiding precept while the operating practice of tenure goes through inevitable change and revision. The most enduring churches understand that the core ideology of the religion must remain fixed while the specific practices and venues of worship change in response to the realities of younger generations. Mission as Drucker thought of it provides the glue that holds an organization together as it expands, decentralizes, globalizes, and attains diversity. Think of it as analogous to the principles of Judaism that held the Jewish people together for centuries without a homeland, even as they scattered throughout the diaspora. Or think of the truths held to be self-evident in the U.S. Declaration of Independence, or the enduring ideals of the scientific community that bond scientists from every nationality together with the common aim of advancing knowledge.

Your core mission provides guidance, not just about what to do but also equally about what *not* to do. Social sector leaders pride themselves on doing good for the world, but to be of maximum service requires a ferocious focus on doing good *only* if it fits your mission. To do the most good requires saying no to pressures to stray and the discipline to stop doing what does not fit. When Frances Hesselbein led the Girl Scouts of the USA, she pounded out a simple mantra: "We are here for only one reason: to help a girl reach her highest potential." She steadfastly steered the Girl Scouts into those activities—and only those activities—that could make a unique and significant contribution of value to its members. When a charity organization sought to collaborate with the Girl Scouts, envisioning an army of smiling girls going door to door to canvass for the greater good, Hesselbein commended the desire to make a difference but gave a polite and firm no. Just because something is a once-in-a-lifetime opportunity—even a once-in-a-lifetime funding opportunity—is merely a fact, not necessarily a reason to act. If a great opportunity does not fit your mission, then the answer must be "Thank you, but no."

The question of mission has become, if anything, even more important as our world becomes increasingly disruptive and turbulent. No matter how much the world changes, people still have a fundamental need to belong to something they can feel proud of. They have a fundamental need for guiding values and sense of purpose that gives their life and work meaning. They have a fundamental need for connection to other people, sharing with them the common bond of beliefs and aspirations. They have a desperate need for a guiding philosophy, a beacon on the hill to keep in sight during dark and disruptive times. More than any time in the past, people will demand operating autonomy—freedom plus responsibility—and will simultaneously demand that the organizations of which they are a part *stand* for something.

WHAT IS YOUR MISSION?
Dr. Marshall Goldsmith and Dr. Kelly Goldsmith

Although much has been written about the *organizational* application of the great question, "What is our mission?" less has been written about the *personal* application.

I (Marshall) had the opportunity to ask Peter F. Drucker his own question. I asked, "Peter, you have spent a lot of your life helping organizations determine their mission. What is *your* mission?"

He replied, "My mission is to help people and organizations achieve their goals." He then laughed and said, "Assuming that they are not immoral or unethical."

Recently, we completed a large study on the relationship of happiness and meaning with both organizational and personal satisfaction with life. What did we learn? In determining a personal mission, you need to make sure that you take into account *both* happiness and meaning.

By *happiness* we are referring to your personal enjoyment of the process itself, not just the results. In other words, at the high end of the scale, you love what you are doing.

By *meaning* we are referring to the value that you attribute to the results of your work. At the high end of the scale, you deeply believe that the outcome of what you are doing is important.

When we asked people to define what happiness and meaning meant to them, we learned that each of us has our own definition and that our personal definition is what matters to us. No one can tell you what makes you happy, and no one can tell you what is meaningful for you. These answers have to come from your heart.

What did our research show? The only way to have high degrees of satisfaction with life at work and at home was to engage in activities that simultaneously produced happiness and meaning.

Participants who reported spending large amounts of time on amusing activities that were fun, but not meaningful, experienced a shallowness in life. They were not highly satisfied with life at work *or* at home. Although we were not surprised about this finding at work, we were a little surprised to see nearly identical results at home. This indicates that an overpreoccupation with amusement may do more harm than good.

Participants who reported spending large amounts of time on meaningful activities that did not produce enjoyment felt like martyrs. Although they believed that what they were doing was important, they were not happy with their lives, either at work or at home.

The only group of respondents in our study who reported consistently high levels of satisfaction with life at work and at home were people who reported that they were spending large amounts of their time on activities that provided simultaneously high levels of happiness and meaning.

Drucker was a wonderful case study of this point. He loved his work and had no interest in retiring. His work made him happy. He also knew that his work mattered. His work gave him meaning. In life, this is the best that we can do.

What are the implications for you?

1. Establish a clear personal mission for yourself. Drucker always said that our mission should be short and clear and that it should "fit on a T-shirt."
2. Make sure that the results you achieve when you succeed in achieving your mission are important to you. Look to your heart. Do what really matters to you.
3. Make sure that the process of achieving your mission is a process that you love. Life is short. Unless your goal is to be a martyr, do what makes you happy.

4.   Another great piece of advice from Drucker is for you to ana-
     lyze how you spend your time. Maximize the amount of time
     that you are experiencing simultaneous happiness and mean-
     ing. To the degree possible, eliminate activities that don't pass
     this test.

The great question, "What is your mission?" is critically
important for organizational success. It may be even more
important for personal success!

MILLENNIAL TAKEAWAY
Michael Radparvar

It was spring 2009 when my brother Dave approached Fabian
and me, suggesting that we take some time to put into words a
reminder of what things exactly were most important to us. Our
company, Holstee, was just three weeks old, we had millions of
things on our plate, and coincidentally we were in the midst of the
worst recession of our generation. Still, we all sensed that putting
this into writing would help us on our journey. Despite the many
things we each had to do for the fledgling company, neither of us
questioned his proposal.

To begin, we agreed that whatever we wrote would be an
important message to our future selves, coming from a time when
our thinking was clear. We also agreed that this would be our best
opportunity to define success in nonfinancial terms. We covered
topics such as love, food, travel, relationships, and our hopes and

dreams. Once we had these most important things charted out, we put them on paper. And for good measure, we decided to put them in a place we knew wouldn't get lost: on the About page of our website, where we called it our manifesto (see Figure 1.1).

Figure 1.1 The Holstee Manifesto

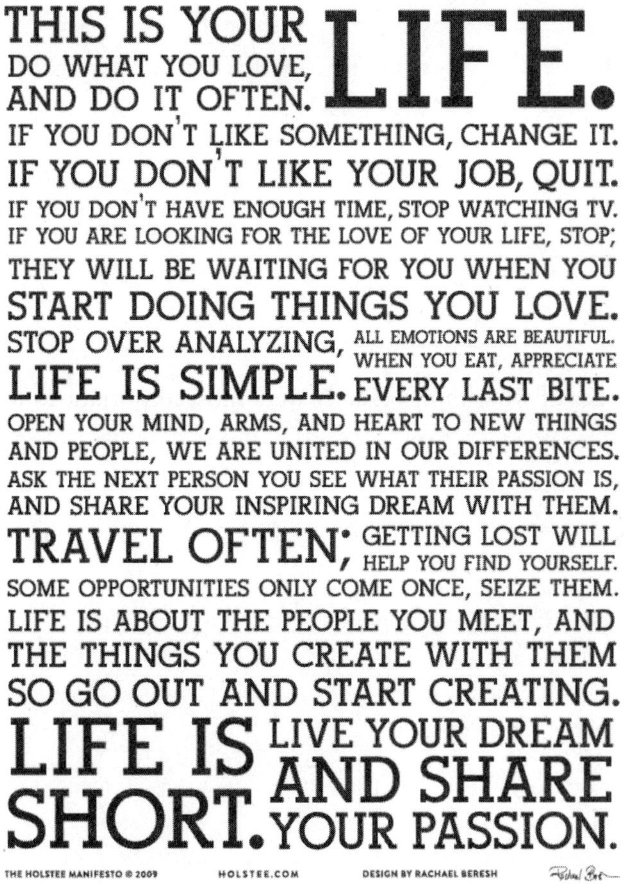

THIS IS YOUR LIFE.
DO WHAT YOU LOVE,
AND DO IT OFTEN.
IF YOU DON'T LIKE SOMETHING, CHANGE IT.
IF YOU DON'T LIKE YOUR JOB, QUIT.
IF YOU DON'T HAVE ENOUGH TIME, STOP WATCHING TV.
IF YOU ARE LOOKING FOR THE LOVE OF YOUR LIFE, STOP;
THEY WILL BE WAITING FOR YOU WHEN YOU
START DOING THINGS YOU LOVE.
STOP OVER ANALYZING, ALL EMOTIONS ARE BEAUTIFUL.
WHEN YOU EAT, APPRECIATE
LIFE IS SIMPLE. EVERY LAST BITE.
OPEN YOUR MIND, ARMS, AND HEART TO NEW THINGS
AND PEOPLE, WE ARE UNITED IN OUR DIFFERENCES.
ASK THE NEXT PERSON YOU SEE WHAT THEIR PASSION IS,
AND SHARE YOUR INSPIRING DREAM WITH THEM.
TRAVEL OFTEN; GETTING LOST WILL
HELP YOU FIND YOURSELF.
SOME OPPORTUNITIES ONLY COME ONCE, SEIZE THEM.
LIFE IS ABOUT THE PEOPLE YOU MEET, AND
THE THINGS YOU CREATE WITH THEM
SO GO OUT AND START CREATING.
LIFE IS LIVE YOUR DREAM
AND SHARE
SHORT. YOUR PASSION.

THE HOLSTEE MANIFESTO © 2009   HOLSTEE.COM   DESIGN BY RACHAEL BERESH

Over the coming months and years, this manifesto took a completely unexpected journey. It grew to become one of the most actively shared images across the Web—and around the world—and it eventually took the form of a letterpress print for better offline sharing as well. In essence, this manifesto also became our company's mission statement. The *Washington Post* referred to it as the "Just Do It" for a new generation. At the core of it all, Holstee's reason to exist—since day one—would simply be to help each of us remember what is important. That to us is the most important thing of all.

WHO IS OUR CUSTOMER?

Peter F. Drucker

- Who is our primary customer?
- Who are our supporting customers?
- How will our customers change?

———

Not long ago, the word *customer* was rarely heard in the social sector. Nonprofit leaders would say, "We don't have customers. That's a marketing term. We have clients . . . recipients . . . patients. We have audience members. We have students." Rather than debate language, I ask, "Who must be satisfied for the organization to achieve results?" When you answer this question, you define your customer as one who values your service, who wants what you offer, who feels it's important to *them*.

Social sector organizations have two types of customers. The *primary* customer is the person whose life is changed through your work. Effectiveness requires focus, and that means *one* response to the question, Who is our primary customer? Those who chase off in too many directions suffer by diffusing their energies and diminishing their performance. *Supporting customers* are volunteers, members, partners, funders, referral sources, employees, and others who must be satisfied. They are all people who can say no, people who have the choice to accept or reject what you offer. You might satisfy them by providing the opportunity for meaningful service, by directing contributions toward results you both believe in, by joining forces to meet community needs.

The primary customer is never the *only* customer, and to satisfy one customer without satisfying the others means there is no performance. This makes it very tempting to say there is more than one primary customer, but effective organizations resist this temptation and keep to a focus—the primary customer.

IDENTIFY THE PRIMARY CUSTOMER

Let me give you a positive example of identifying and concentrating on the primary customer in a complex setting. A mid-sized nonprofit organization's mission is *to increase people's economic and social independence*. They have twenty-five programs considered to be in four different fields, but for thirty-five years they have focused on only one primary customer: *the person with multiple barriers to employment*. In the beginning, this meant the physically handicapped. Today, it still means people with disabilities but also single mothers who want to be finished with welfare, older workers who have been laid off, people with chronic and persistent mental illness living in the community, and those struggling against long-term chemical dependency. Each belongs to a single primary customer group: the person with multiple barriers to employment. Results are measured in every program by whether the customer can now gain and keep productive work.

The primary customer is not necessarily someone you can reach, someone you can sit down with and talk to directly. Primary customers may be infants, or endangered species, or members of a future generation. Whether or not you can have an active dialogue, identifying the primary customer puts your priorities in order and gives you a reference point for critical decisions on the organization's values.

IDENTIFYING SUPPORTING CUSTOMERS

The Girl Scouts of United States of America is the largest girls' and women's organization in the world and a nonprofit that exemplifies service to one primary customer—the girl—balanced with satisfaction of many supporting customers, all of whom change over time. A long-held Girl Scouts priority is offering equal access to every girl in the United States. This has not changed since 1912 when the Girl Scouts founder said, "I have something for all the girls." Frances Hesselbein, at the time she was national executive director (1976–1990), told me, "We look at the projections and understand that by the year 2000, one-third of this country will be members of minority groups. Many people are very apprehensive about the future and what this new racial and ethnic composition will mean. We see it as an unprecedented opportunity to reach all girls with a program that will help them in their growing-up years, which are more difficult than ever before."

Reaching a changing primary customer means a new view of supporting customers. Frances explained, "In a housing project with no Girl Scout troop there are hundreds of young girls really needing this kind of program, and families wanting something better for their children. It is important as we reach out to girls in every racial and economic group to understand the very special needs, the culture, the readiness of each group. We work with many supporting customers; with the clergy perhaps, with the director of that housing project, with parents—a group of people from that particular community. We recruit leaders, train them right there. We have to demonstrate our respect for that community, our interest in it. Parents have to know it will be a positive experience for their daughters."

KNOW YOUR CUSTOMERS

Customers are never static. There will be greater or lesser numbers in the groups you already serve. They will become more diverse. Their needs, wants, and aspirations will evolve. There may be entirely new customers you must satisfy to achieve results—individuals who really need the service, want the service, but not in the way in which it is available today. And there are customers you should *stop* serving because the organization has filled a need, because people can be better served elsewhere, or because you are not producing results.

Answering the question Who is our customer? provides the basis for determining what customers value, defining your results, and developing the plan. Yet, even after careful thought, customers may surprise you; then you must be prepared to adjust. I remember one of my pastoral friends saying of a new program, "Great, a wonderful program for the newly married." The program was indeed a success. But to the consternation of the young assistant pastor who designed it and ran it, not a single newly married couple enrolled. All the participants were young people living together and wondering whether they should get married. And the senior pastor had a terrible time with his brilliant young assistant, who became righteous and said, "We haven't designed it for them!" He wanted to throw them out.

Often, the customer is one step ahead of you. So you must *know your customer*—or quickly get to know them. Time and again you will have to ask, "Who is our customer?" because customers constantly change. The organization that is devoted to results—always with regard to its basic integrity—will adapt and change as they do.[1]

WHO IS OUR CUSTOMER?

Philip Kotler

Peter F. Drucker told us more than 40 years ago, "The purpose of a company is to create a customer . . . The only profit center is the customer." Jack Welch, former chief executive officer of General Electric, drove the same point home to his employees: "Nobody can guarantee your job. Only customers can guarantee your job." In the Internet age, when customers have so much more information and are daily exchanging opinions with each other, companies are finally waking up to the idea that they have a new boss: the customer. A perceptive Ford executive at one time said, "If we're not customer driven, our cars won't be either."

If Peter Drucker were here today, he would amend his observation. He would say, "The best companies don't create customers. They create fans." He would say that it is less important to report better profits this year than to check on whether you improved your share of the customer's mind and heart this year.

We must do a better job of understanding who the customer is. The old thinking was that customers would hear about us and, we hope, choose our products. The new thinking is that we, the company, choose our customers. We even may refuse to do business with certain customers. Our business is not to please everyone casually but to please our target customers deeply.

So the first job is to define our target customers. This definition will affect everything: the designing of our product and its features, the choice of our distribution outlets, the crafting of our messages, the choice of our media, and the setting of our prices.

To define our customer, we must take a broader view of the buying process. The purchase of anything is the result of several roles being played. Consider the purchase of a new family automobile. The *initiator* might have been a family friend who mentioned an impressive new car. The teenage son might have been an *influencer* of the type of car to consider. The *decider* might be the wife. The *buyer* might be the husband.

The marketer's job is to identify these roles and use the limited marketing resources to reach the most influential people involved in the final decision. Marketers and salespeople need skills in mapping the perceptions, preferences, and values of the different players in the decision-making process.

Many companies have adopted *customer relationship management,* meaning that they collect loads of information about transactions and encounters with their customers. Most pharmaceutical firms, for example, have deep information on individual physicians and their values and preferences. Increasingly, however, we are recognizing that this information is not enough. It doesn't capture the quality of the *customer experience.* Simply managing data about customers is no substitute for ensuring that the customers are satisfied with their experience of the company. An old Chinese proverb says, "If you cannot smile, do not open a shop."

So in the end, we must master our knowledge of who the target customers are, who and what influences them, and how to create highly satisfying customer experiences. Recognize that today's customers are increasingly buying on value, not on relationship. Your success ultimately depends on what you have contributed to the success of your customers.

CUSTOMERS AT THE CENTER OF EVERYTHING!

Raghu Krishnamoorthy

In early July 2014, tucked away in the labor section of *Bloomberg Businessweek,* was an article by Josh Eidelson titled "Uber: The

Company Cities Love to Hate." Uber is a relatively new and direct competitor to the well-established, taxi-based transportation model in cities around the world. It has been a major disrupter to the stronghold of the age-old taxi, with its cattle car–like interiors, overpriced rides, extra charges for credit card payments, and so on. No-brainer, if you ask me to choose between an Uber car and a taxi. You use your Uber app to call a clean, timely, professional-looking driver and car, pay through the app, and with no tip expected and predictable charges, you feel comfortable, safe, and assured of the service. Of course, the traditional taxi drivers are outraged, and some cities have even banned Uber because it is threatening the well-oiled machine of mediocrity.

But ask the customers, and they will swear by Uber. They love the convenience, quality, hassle-free, predictable nature of the service that Uber provides. So why shouldn't they use Uber?

The *Bloomberg Businessweek* article reported a $17 billion valuation for Uber. If, as Peter Drucker says, "the purpose of a business is to create a customer," Uber has hit the mark squarely. It has actually created fans, not just customers.

Uber, Airbnb, Cree, Rent the Runway, Amazon.com, Google, and Facebook are all new age examples of how customer-first thinking has become *the* business model, not a part of it. So much so, they are having a tremendous impact on the *concept* of business . . . period.

If Drucker were alive today, he perhaps would have had a sense of déjà vu! When Drucker first emphasized that the customer was the center of business strategy, he was ahead of his time in some ways. In an era dominated by the fact that creating shareholder value was considered the purpose of a business model, he was almost prophetic in insisting on customers being placed at the epicenter of an organizational purpose. Now, that philosophy seems obvious. Organizations, big and small, old and new, global and local, have to think of their businesses as in service to the customers and build their value proposition around it. Everything else, including shareholder value, is a consequence and a derivative of that fundamental truth. Bottom line, Drucker is astoundingly more relevant today than ever. He was a Millennial in his thinking before we knew of the Millennials.

Here is the interesting thing. Drucker's perspectives were so far-reaching that he did not just stop with his spotlight on the customer; he went on to warn that the notion of the customer is not a static one—and that organizations need to be prepared for customers becoming more diverse, with their needs, wants, and aspirations continuously evolving over time. In this shape-shifting world of customers, he argued, a company's success therefore depends on its contribution to its customers' success. Keeping a close pulse on this dynamic world of customers will be key to a company's survival—otherwise it runs the risk of becoming irrelevant, and therefore, redundant.

General Electric (GE) is a 130-plus-year-old company. As the only company still on the original Dow Jones index, it has stayed relevant primarily because it has successfully morphed and kept itself young and fresh over its long history. Thomas Edison, the founder of GE, not only invented the lightbulb (and a multitude of other things) but also literally invented invention. No organization survives because of its products alone but stays alive because it invents and innovates constantly its organizational processes to surround the products. In some ways, the greatest innovations of the twenty-first century are not going to be about products or technology but about how we organize ourselves to deliver value to the customers. At GE, reimagining and reinventing ourselves to stay contemporary to our customers' needs is a part of the DNA. In other words, GE has always pursued Drucker's caution of "planned abandonment" to evolve.

Drucker's emphasis that "planning is not masterminding the future" but "in the face of uncertainties, planning defines the particular place you want to be and *how* you intend to get there" becomes a guidepost for organizational strategy and direction. The concept and the relevance of the customer that Drucker emphasized has become a lot more pronounced in today's world, making his statement timeless and oracle-like. What has changed is how we get there based on shifts that have happened in this century. These shifts, such as the ones in technology disruption, the migration from the information to the social era, demographic shifts (primarily the Millennials versus the baby boomers) leading to psychographic differences, and so on, are well documented and now part of the popular management theory today. What is not as well known is how organizations are migrating to meet this brave new world. And no, not organizations such as Uber or Airbnb, not even Google and Facebook, because these are products of the new era anyway but organizations such as GE and others that have the ability to rise irrespective of the contexts they live in.

At GE, Chairman Jeff Immelt is driving an initiative called simplification, a way of bringing about a small company mind-set in a big company body. Being in more than 170 countries in a range of businesses from lightbulbs to jet engines, understanding the needs of target customers, and figuring out how to respond quickly is the name of the game.

There are four key elements of simplification:

1. *Lean management*: This directly takes the start-up toolkit and brings it into an organization like GE. The mind-set change required is that we need to be agile, nimble, and willing to experiment and learn to grow. It is a way of testing what Drucker questions, "do we... or can we produce sufficiently outstanding results to justify putting resources in this area," and if we don't, can we change directions (called pivoting)? Lean management calls for customers to be at the center of every decision—and have them be not just a recipient of our products and services but also a participant in the process. Lean management also has the urging to be intense, austere, and focused.

2. *Commercial and customer intensity*: This part of simplification addresses the "getting to yes" for the customer. How do we organize ourselves to make sure that we deliver when, where, and how the customer wants products and services? Furthermore, how do we anticipate, analyze, and offer solutions to our customers so that we deeply please the target customer base? This means the organizational model is far more front-end oriented, and everyone and every process aligns to make the front-end interface to the customer be an outstanding experience. Moments of truth with the customer are translated

into organizational measures of success. Data on products and services become gold mines of insight so that the commercial teams offer solutions ahead of the need, not as a reaction to the customer need. Commercial capabilities, organizational models, and measures of success, as well as data capabilities, are being retooled at GE to ride this change.

3. *A services focus*: Increasingly, in a complex world, people look at products as a means to an end—and knowing the "end" and figuring out the value proposition around that is critical for success. For instance, you are not buying jet engines to power the airplane anymore; you are buying fuel efficiency. You are not buying a lightbulb but rather durability. You are going to the hospital to prevent diseases from happening, not just to cure what you already have. Value, therefore, has to be translated from the mind-set of the product to the mind-set of the customer. What does the customer want to solve for? Adding the variety of service innovation to surround the product innovation is what is going to be an increased differentiator. iTunes is the differentiator to the iPod, apps are the differentiator to the smartphone, and likewise offering live data feeds on an airplane's path and using them to proactively prevent untoward accidents and incidents could be incredibly valuable.

4. *Technology*: Perhaps the biggest lever that is available these days is the phenomenal world of technology. Cloud-based technology, the industrial Internet, the Internet of things, additive manufacturing, industrial automation, and other innovations have made available a range of tools to companies to make products and services faster, smarter, and cheaper.

GE has invested heavily in these areas and is able to deliver unique value to the customers. For instance, the light emitting diode (LED) bulb that you can shut off and on remotely through your smart device is a simple example of the marriage of technology with traditional hardware, creating interesting permutations and combinations that would otherwise not be possible.

In a corporation, the ultimate truth—the ultimate measure— is determined by the customer. Drucker was a pioneer in propounding the focus on the customer. Today we are seeing the benefit of that. Organizations form to rise to the challenge of an unmet need. As Drucker prophesized, the ultimate beneficiary is the customer. Drucker went on to promise that those organizations that rise to the challenge will have the capability to be responsive to customer feedback, look within constantly, drive innovation, and embrace change.

At GE, we encapsulate this constant flow of change in a telling phrase: Together, we all rise! Because we have no doubts—when we solve for the customer, he or she rises, and when he or she does, so do we.

MILLENNIAL TAKEAWAY

Luke Owings

When Peter F. Drucker asked the question "Who is our customer?" he focused on the primary customer, and it's quite likely that this highly visible group inspired you as a young person to join your company. However, in many jobs, your main interface is actually not with primary customers but with customers who play a supporting role. By thinking of the supporting customers whom you *do* work with, you can fuel both the organization and your own connection to the mission.

At the Fullbridge Program, I maintained a network of independent contractors to coach our month-long business boot camps. Each year, we'd hire dozens of highly skilled business-people to use our materials and mentor business neophytes at the start of their careers. By standardizing tasks and styles (the handbook approach, if you will), we achieved an outcome that was both consistent and repeatable. However, this top-down approach created inflexibility and only marginal improvement from delivery to delivery.

Recognizing that the independent contractors attracted to Fullbridge were both transitioning in their careers and interested in creating more value, we modified our approach to these engagements. By being clear on what *had* to be done—and removing all unessential tasks—we encouraged them to cultivate their own approaches and we focused our management on their professional development. Consequently, our products better served our primary customers, and our independent contractors more effectively shaped pedagogy and curriculum to delivery and marketing.

The supporting customers of the future are groups like these independent contractors living so-called mosaic careers.

As networking tools proliferate, the market of short-term engagements is exploding. Companies adept at tapping these growing pools will harness their volatility into a strong source of innovation. Only by recognizing the needs and motivations of collaborators will you create a system that propels forward the mission (and primary customers) that inspired you in the first place.

WHAT DOES THE CUSTOMER VALUE?

Peter F. Drucker

- What do we believe our primary and supporting customers value?
- What knowledge do we need to gain from our customers?
- How will I participate in gaining this knowledge?

———

The question, What do customers value?—what satisfies their needs, wants, and aspirations—is so complicated that it can only be answered by customers themselves. And the first rule is that there are no irrational customers. Almost without exception, customers behave rationally in terms of their own realities and their own situation. Leadership should not even try to guess at the answers but should always go to the customers in a systematic quest for those answers. I practice this. Each year

I personally telephone a random sample of fifty or sixty students who graduated ten years earlier. I ask, "Looking back, what did we contribute in this school? What is still important to you? What should we do better? What should we stop doing?" And believe me, the knowledge I have gained has had a profound influence.

What does the customer value? may be the most important question. Yet it is the one least often asked. Nonprofit leaders tend to answer it for themselves. "It's the quality of our programs. It's the way we improve the community." People are so convinced they are doing the right things and so committed to their cause that they come to see the institution as an end in itself. But that's a bureaucracy. Instead of asking, "Does it deliver value to our customers?" they ask, "Does it fit our rules?" And that not only inhibits performance but also destroys vision and dedication.

UNDERSTAND YOUR ASSUMPTIONS

My friend Philip Kotler, a professor at Northwestern University, points out that many organizations are very clear about the value they would like to deliver, but they often don't understand that value from the perspective of their customers. They make assumptions based on their own interpretation. So begin with assumptions and find out what *you* believe your customers value. Then you can compare these beliefs with what customers actually are saying, find the differences, and go on to assess your results.

WHAT DOES THE PRIMARY CUSTOMER VALUE?

Learning what their primary customers value led to significant change in a homeless shelter. The shelter's existing beliefs about value added up to nutritious meals and clean beds. A series of face-to-face interviews with their homeless customers was arranged, and both board and staff members took part. They found out that yes, the food and beds are appreciated but do little or nothing to satisfy the deep aspiration *not to be homeless*. The customers said, "We need a place of safety from which to rebuild our lives, a place we can at least temporarily call a real home." The organization threw out their assumptions and their old rules. They said, "How can we make this shelter a safe haven?" They eliminated the fear that comes with being turned back on the street each morning. They now make it possible to stay at the shelter quite a while, and work with individuals to find out what a rebuilt life means to them and how they can be helped to realize their goal.

The new arrangement also requires more of the customer. Before, it was enough to show up hungry. Now, to get what the customer values most, he must make a commitment. He must work on his problems and plans in order to stay on. The customer's stake in the relationship is greater, as are the organization's results.

WHAT DO SUPPORTING CUSTOMERS VALUE?

Your knowledge of what primary customers value is of utmost importance. Yet the reality is, unless you understand equally what supporting customers value, you will not be able to put all the necessary pieces in place for the organization to perform. In social sector organizations there have always been a multitude of supporting customers, in some cases each with a veto power. A school principal has to satisfy teachers, the school board, community partners, the taxpayers, parents, and above all, the primary customer—the young student. The principal has six constituencies, each of which sees the school differently. Each of them is essential, each defines value differently, and each has to be satisfied at least to the point where they don't fire the principal, go on strike, or rebel.

LISTEN TO YOUR CUSTOMERS

To formulate a successful plan you will need to understand each of your constituencies' concerns, especially what they consider results in the long term. Integrating what customers value into the institution's plan is almost an architectural process, a structural process. It's not too difficult to do once it's understood, but it's hard work. First, think through what knowledge you need to gain. Then listen to customers, accept what they value as objective fact, and make sure the customer's voice is part of your discussions and decisions, not just during the self-assessment process, but continually.[1]

WHAT DOES THE CUSTOMER VALUE?

Jim Kouzes

Everything exemplary leaders do is about creating value for their customers.

That is exactly the perspective Patricia Maryland, now president, Healthcare Operations and COO of Ascension Health, took when she came on board as president of Sinai-Grace Hospital in Detroit, Michigan. When Maryland arrived, she found a hospital in distress. Sinai-Grace was the one hospital remaining after a series of mergers, and all the "slashing and burning" had left the staff feeling angry and distrustful. But even after all the cuts, the hospital was still losing money. Sinai-Grace was an organization not only looking for new leadership but also searching for a new identity.

One of the first things Maryland noticed was that employees mostly related to the way things had been done in the past and that breaking this deep-seated paradigm would be one of the first tasks she and her team needed to tackle. For example, one obvious challenge was the long waits that patients—the hospital's customers—experienced in the emergency room (ER). "When I first came here, it took people an average of 8 hours to be seen and admitted to a hospital bed," Maryland said, "and this was clearly unacceptable."

Another challenge was the way the community perceived the hospital. According to Maryland, there were individuals who lived within a block of us who tended to go to other hospitals.

It was clear that the physical environment was a big part of the problem. These long-standing and accepted issues demanded immediate action, and resolving them required experimenting with fundamentally new approaches.

To address the unacceptable ER wait times, the team challenged the hospital's traditional departmental structure. A separate area for chest pain patients was created so patients would be triaged immediately, and the urgent care population was moved to another area called Express Care. In Express Care, the hospital built examination rooms with walls, improving privacy and confidentiality. These simple changes reduced wait time by more than 75 percent.

Building on this success was a $100,000 foundation grant to upgrade hospital decor. Fresh paint, new carpets, and new furniture can do wonders for the morale of both patients and staff. Doctors donated artwork, and the environment took an immediate turn for the better, beginning to look like a contemporary medical center. "I really felt it was important to create an environment here that was warm, that was embracing, that would allow patients coming in the door to feel some level of trust and comfort," Maryland explained.

The staff was also challenged to look at the way they related to patients: "If this was your mother or your father, how would you work with them? How would you talk to them? How would you feel if someone was cold, unfriendly, and treated you like you're a piece of machinery rather than a human being?"

These first few changes at Sinai-Grace Hospital started an outstanding turnaround. Customer service scores went up dramatically—from mostly 1s and 2s on a 5-point scale to mostly

4s and 5s. Today staff morale is high, and there's a new vitality and enthusiasm at Sinai-Grace. And the hospital is now doing quite well financially. Most important, said Maryland, "There's confidence from the community, and they are feeling more comfortable coming back here."

An unyielding commitment to listening to and creating value for the customer drove all these improvements. It was Maryland's dedication to first understanding how the hospital's customers experienced Sinai-Grace and then responding to their needs—and enabling staff to do the same—that supported each innovation to restore the health and well-being of the organization and the morale and pride of the staff. All of this was possible because the entire team, with Maryland leading from the front, not pushing from the back, had one fundamental purpose in mind: to create extraordinary value for the customer.

So, what does the customer value? Clearly customers value an organization that seeks their feedback and that is capable of solving their problems and meeting their needs. But I would also venture to guess that customers value a leader and a team who have the ability to listen and the courage to challenge the business-as-usual environment, all in service of the yearnings of the customer.

CREATING CUSTOMER VALUE: HOW WELL IS YOUR BRAND HELPING CUSTOMERS?

Michael and Kass Lazerow

Welcome to the customer revolution, where you are no longer in charge.

Social networks, mobile devices, connected products, and cloud computing have forever changed your relationship with your customers and potential customers.

The customer revolution is a radical shift of power from companies to their connected customers. Armed with one's phone, the power and influence of each customer is contained only by the size and influence of his or her network.

The customer revolution is a quiet revolution. Billions of people influence their family, friends, and colleagues seamlessly thanks to text messages, Facebook, Twitter, Pinterest, and other social apps.

Companies that ride this revolution will thrive. Companies that stick their heads in the sand will die. Yes, it's that binary.

So how does your company join the customer revolution?

Simple—by connecting in a whole new way. And the most powerful way to do that is to help your customers every step of the way in their journey with you.

Yes, to connect is to help. That's not a new concept. What's new is that companies need to provide that help *when* the customer wants and *how* the customer wants that help provided. And it's never been a more exciting time to do just that.

Yesterday, customers needed to go into a store for help. Yesterday, customers needed to do it at the time the company said (9 AM to 5 PM) and at their own expense.

Today, customers expect to be helped at the time when *they* want to be helped and on *their* terms. Companies that get this are already reaching new heights and many are revolutionizing their industries.

Take Uber, whose mobile app is blowing up the local transportation business today and most likely more in the future. Its stats are staggering.

It now serves 43 percent of the U.S. population—all without owning any vehicles! Uber is creating the equivalent of about 20,000 jobs every month. And in our hometown of New York City, each of those jobs generates a median income of more than $90,000 a year. A *Business Wire* press release estimated that Uber contributes $2.8 billion to the U.S. economy every year.

All of this is made possible because of the mobile phone and cloud computing. Without mobile devices, there's no Uber.

The help Uber provides is simple: We need to get from here to there. That help is provided when we want it: We need a ride now! And the help is provided how we want it: Press a button and the car comes to us! Date night will never be the same!

This framework is why Uber, which was not around a few years ago, now generates hundreds of millions in revenues and was recently valued by smart, professional investors at $18 billion.

Let's take another industry, automobiles. In the past, the red light would go off in the car, and you would freak out, not knowing what was going on. You would reach for the manual and try to figure it out. You wouldn't figure it out. So you would spend 30 minutes making an appointment to bring it in to the dealer for service. You would miss an hour of work dropping the car off and then another hour later in the day picking it up.

So you're getting the help you need—but not when you need it or on your terms.

Now almost every new car is connected to the network. Tomorrow, when something breaks, a message will pop up on the dashboard that says, "Hi Mike and Kass. You have driven 8,000 miles on your filter. It's time to change it. Press this button to schedule the appointment." The dealer will come to you to pick up the car and then drop it off when it's done. Why? Customers will expect that thanks to all the on-demand products and services willing to provide that level of help.

What we are witnessing is the rapid convergence of sales, service, and marketing. Every interaction with a customer is now marketing. Marketing was once focused on the destination—and that destination was most likely a purchase. Marketing is now about the customer journey, and customers expect you to be there to help them every step of the way—before, during, and after the purchase.

We buy products because they help us in some way. We now expect that help is delivered on our terms.

Welcome to the customer revolution, where *customers* are now in charge.

MILLENNIAL TAKEAWAY
Nadira Hira

It's so tempting to believe that we know better than ever before what our customers value. In these connected times—a twenty-first-century world where I can tweet @Delta about a travel problem before my fellow fliers even figure out where to line up with questions—organizations, brands, and leaders all have access to a constant stream of feedback.

But do we use it effectively?

I can't count the number of times an executive has told me, laughing, that he's "got no idea" about Twitter. Or confessed how annoyed she is by flip comments on the company's Facebook page or Instagram feed. Or, perhaps worst of all, shared with pride that their organizations are directly plugged in to what customers want because of, well, social media!

We are in a moment of unprecedented consumer engagement tools. But the tools themselves are nothing more and nothing less than how we use them. Ignore them, and you're missing a tremendous opportunity. Exalt them too much, though—relying solely on whatever insight they provide—and you'll likely see only the barest contours of your customers' wants, needs, and frustrations.

So take a lesson from one of the industries I've most enjoyed covering: innovation. It's common wisdom in this field that customers don't actually know what they want. But that isn't innovation practitioners denigrating consumers; it's an example of dedicated professionals reminding themselves that, when it comes to providing the very best product or service, they should never stop at the first, simplest, or most available answer. They dig; they frame, and reframe; they explore all the angles they can imagine to help customers discover deeper truths about their ideal experience. From taking quick advantage of every bit of technology around, to doing as Peter F. Drucker did decades ago—talking, live and in earnest, to real customers old and new—they *interrogate*.

That's our challenge as leaders, and if we meet it, there's no limit to what we can do for those people who honor us with their business.

QUESTION 4

WHAT ARE OUR RESULTS?

Peter F. Drucker

- How do we define results?
- Are we successful?
- How should we define results?
- What must we strengthen or abandon?

The results of social sector organizations are always measured *outside* the organization in changed lives and changed conditions—in people's behavior, circumstances, health, hopes, and above all, in their competence and capacity. To further the mission, each nonprofit needs to determine what should be appraised and judged, then concentrate resources for results.

LOOK AT SHORT-TERM ACCOMPLISHMENTS AND LONG-TERM CHANGE

A small mental health center was founded and directed by a dedicated husband-and-wife team, both psychotherapists. They called it a "healing community," and in the fifteen years they ran the organization, they achieved results others had dismissed as impossible. Their primary customers were people diagnosed with schizophrenia, and most came to the center following failure after failure in treatment, their situation nearly hopeless.

The people at the center said, "There *is* somewhere to turn." Their first measure was whether primary customers and their families were willing to try again. The staff had a number of ways to monitor progress. Did participants regularly attend group sessions and participate fully in daily routines? Did the incidence and length of psychiatric hospitalizations decrease? Could these individuals show new understanding of their disease by saying, "I have had an episode," as opposed to citing demons in the closet? As they progressed, could participants set realistic goals for their own next steps?

The center's mission was *to enable people with serious and persistent mental illness to recover,* and after two or more years of intensive work, many could function in this world—they were no longer "incurable." Some were able to return to a life with their family. Others could hold steady jobs. A few completed graduate school. Whether or not members of that healing community did recover—whether the lives of primary customers changed in this fundamental way—was the organization's single bottom line.

In business, you can debate whether profit is really an adequate measuring stick, but without it, there *is* no business in the long term. In the social sector, no such universal standard for success exists. Each organization must identify its customers, learn what they value, develop meaningful measures, and honestly judge whether, in fact, lives are being changed. This is a new discipline for many nonprofit groups, but it is one that can be learned.

QUALITATIVE AND QUANTITATIVE MEASURES

Progress and achievement can be appraised in *qualitative* and *quantitative* terms. These two types of measures are interwoven— they shed light on one another—and both are necessary to illuminate in what ways and to what extent lives are being changed.

Qualitative measures address the depth and breadth of change within its particular context. They begin with specific observations, build toward patterns, and tell a subtle, individualized story. Qualitative appraisal offers valid, "rich" data. The education director at a major museum tells of the man who sought her out to explain how the museum had opened his teenage mind to new possibilities in a way he knew literally saved his life. She used this result to support her inspiration for a new initiative with troubled youth. The people in a successful research institute cannot quantify the value of their research ahead of time. But they can sit down every three years and ask, "What have we achieved that contributed to changed lives? Where do we focus now for results tomorrow?" Qualitative results can be in the realm of the intangible, such as instilling hope in a patient battling cancer. Qualitative data, although sometimes more subjective and difficult to grasp, are just as real, just as important, and can be gathered just as systematically as the quantitative.

Quantitative measures use definitive standards. They begin with categories and expectations and tell an objective story. Quantitative appraisal offers valid "hard" data. Examples of quantitative measures are as follows: whether overall school performance improves when at-risk youth have intensive arts education; whether the percentage of welfare recipients who complete training and become employed at a livable wage goes up; whether health professionals change their practice based on new research; whether the number of teenagers who smoke goes up or down; whether incidences of child abuse fall when twenty-four-hour crisis care is available. Quantitative measures are essential for assessing whether resources are properly concentrated for results, whether progress is being made, whether lives and communities are changing for the better.

ASSESS WHAT MUST BE STRENGTHENED OR ABANDONED

One of the most important questions for nonprofit leadership is, Do we produce results that are sufficiently outstanding for us to

justify putting our resources in this area? Need alone does not justify continuing. Nor does tradition. You must match your mission,
your concentration, and your results. Like the New Testament
parable of the talents, your job is to invest your resources where
the returns are manifold, where you can have success.

To abandon anything is always bitterly resisted. People in any
organization are always attached to the obsolete—the things that
should have worked but did not, the things that once were productive and no longer are. They are most attached to what in an
earlier book (*Managing for Results,* 1964) I called "investments in
managerial ego." Yet abandonment comes first. Until that has been
accomplished, little else gets done. The acrimonious and emo-
tional debate over what to abandon holds everybody in its grip.
Abandoning anything is thus difficult, but only for a fairly short
spell. Rebirth can begin once the dead are buried; six months later,
everybody wonders, "Why did it take us so long?"

LEADERSHIP IS ACCOUNTABLE

There are times to face the fact that the organization as a whole is
not performing—that there are weak results everywhere and little
prospect of improving. It may be time to merge or liquidate and
put your energies somewhere else. And in some performance areas,
whether to strengthen or abandon is not clear. You will need a
systematic analysis as part of your plan.

At this point in the self-assessment process, you determine
what results for the organization should be and where to concentrate for future success. The mission defines the scope of your

responsibility. Leadership is accountable to determine what must be appraised and judged, to protect the organization from squandering resources, and to ensure meaningful results.[1]

WHAT ARE OUR RESULTS?

Dr. Judith Rodin

Peter F. Drucker wrote that the "most exciting" development in his half century of work with nonprofits was that they had begun to talk not of *needs* but of *results*. This was progress of a very important sort—and Drucker, typically, understated his own role in helping inspire the change.

Drucker's explication of question 4 clearly and cogently lays out some of the most important subordinate questions in the evaluation of outcomes in the nonprofit sector: What are the prerequisites for our success? How do our partners and beneficiaries experience our work? What are our qualitative as well as quantitative goals? How do we define our results? Do we have the courage to admit failure and let others learn from our mistakes?

I would submit, however, that Drucker's insights in this matter are now sufficiently well understood that he would want us today to go further. The contemporary discussion around evaluation is no longer whether it is worthwhile—it surely is; nor is it around whether quantitative measurements alone are sufficient—surely they are not; nor is it confined to whether failure is admissible—surely we must admit that human efforts, no matter how well intended, must fall short and that refusal to admit failure and share the knowledge with others only compounds that failure.

Instead, the next question—question 4A, if you will—asks us how we use our results to play a role in Drucker's question 5, "What is our plan?"

The Five Most Important Questions proceeds on the implicit premise that our plan is fixed and that the results must flow from it. But the program work of a nonprofit is more iterative than linear. Our plan needs to be designed not only to further our mission but also *to yield measurable results* so that we can know whether the plan is succeeding. Just as Drucker is correct in observing that needs are not enough, that intentions are insufficient, it is also true that a plan should not be considered complete, or even satisfactory, until it has been constructed in such a way as to produce some measurable outcomes and to build mechanisms, a priori, that allow midcourse corrections based on these results. This work is not like conducting a clinical trial or a randomized controlled experiment, however, where we do not break the code until the end. The goal is to achieve real impact; thus, measuring results is a tool for learning, for self-correcting, to reach intended, specified outcomes.

In saying this, we must sail between two shoals, what we might think of as the Scylla and Charybdis of nonprofit planning. On one hand, we must ensure that our plans are designed in such a way that results are measurable. If necessary to guarantee this, we must even be willing to alter our choices of specific interventions to undertake, avoiding those where, for instance, the defined impact is so unclear and immeasurable as to be beyond our reach. On the other hand, we must also avoid the other shoal—the temptation to undertake only that work most easily quantified, to choose the sort of task that produces outputs but fails to alter the most important outcomes. In this way, to pursue the metaphor just one phrase further, our voyage is an artistic and not just scientific endeavor.

Drucker begins his discussion of question 4 by observing, with emphasis in the original, that *"results are the key to our survival"* as institutions. If results are our goal, they must also be our test. What endures from the work of nonprofits is not how hard we try, how clever we may be, or even how much we care. Hard work is indispensable to success, of course, in this as in any other field; intelligence is prized in our sector as in all others involving intellectual endeavor; and caring is what has drawn the best people into this line of work. And our offerings must appeal and be relevant to a younger generation of patrons, volunteers, and donors, for without the revitalizing force of new members from the communities in which these organizations reside, nonprofits risk calcifying and losing the ability to sustain themselves. But ultimately what is remembered is how we have been able to improve lives. Drucker understood this profoundly. This is why his question, "What are our results?" resonates today.

WHAT ARE OUR RESULTS?

Col. Bernard Banks

All organizations exist to produce outcomes. Such outcomes are generated in variety of forms (e.g., products sold, services provided, net income achieved, dollars raised, and students taught). Regardless of type, developing an understanding of what any result really means is a very important leadership activity. Peter F. Drucker highlighted the importance of understanding results within his iconic five questions one should ask about his or her organization. However, my reflections concerning in particular Drucker's question, "What are our results?" have led me to conclude that an additional filter is necessary to consider when evaluating the things one measures. Therefore, I submit that leaders must also examine results through the prism of organizational and personal values.

Drucker's Pillars of How to Examine Results

Obviously, organizations must be cognizant as to whether they are achieving the right outcomes. Failure to evaluate critically the outputs an enterprise's activities produce can lead to skewed perceptions and potentially extinction. Consequently, Drucker highlighted several illuminating questions designed to foster a more comprehensive examination of outcomes (e.g., How do we define success? Are we successful? How should we define results? What must we strengthen or abandon?). The variety of Drucker's espoused reflection was crafted to examine short- and long-term outcomes through different types of data (i.e., quantitative and qualitative). Breadth and depth generally yield a better understanding of any phenomenon. Yet, it is natural to wonder whether Drucker's concise framework provided us all the prompts one should take into account when examining results. Leaders' ability to develop an accurate understanding of organizational efforts matters because of one important outcome—influence.

The ultimate impact of exploring outcomes is influence. Organizations' future behavior is generally influenced by the success or failure associated with their previous endeavors. Organizations and leaders inherently understand the need to get things right. Drucker once noted, "*results are the key to our survival.*" But, is it possible to get seemingly positive results the wrong way? I contend the answer is yes.

The Importance of a Values Filter

Values are designed to serve as individuals and organizations' "true north."[2] It is a rare organization that has not taken the time to establish some set of formal values. Yet, all too often organizations do not examine their actions through the lens such espoused statements of beliefs and principles provide. Failure to do so introduces needless risk into their future undertakings. The U.S. Army says its values "consist of the principles, standards and qualities considered essential for successful Army leaders. They are fundamental to helping Soldiers and Army Civilians make the right decision in any situation."[3] So, why must one examine values in concert with results? One story immediately comes to mind.

When I was attending a graduate program several years ago, I had a professor who had just finished a very successful tenure as the chief executive officer (CEO) of a Fortune 500 company. One day in class we were discussing leaders' responsibilities for influencing their organizations' business practices. Several students were intent on highlighting the need always to maximize share-holder value. Suddenly, the professor began to tell a story about an acquisition that his company had elected not to pursue. He said his firm had identified an opportunity that held tremendous potential to generate significant profit. However, acquiring the targeted entity would require laying off significant numbers of people and selling big pieces of the enterprise to harvest their economic value. Subsequently, many communities would face an immediate downturn because of the proposed action. The CEO mulled over the opportunity and decided not to do it. Consequently, he informed the company's board and his senior leadership team that pursuing the proposed acquisition made sense on paper. However, it did not withstand the scrutiny of the company's values. So, the deal never transpired. If the CEO had considered the potential financial results only, a very different outcome might have transpired.

The Prism of Your Beliefs

Leaders and organizations are entrusted with influencing people's lives. Long-term vitality for each of the aforementioned groups is contingent upon delivering the right results at the right time. Results matter! However, how one generates results also matters. Drucker's five questions continue to serve as an invaluable resource for helping create clarity of perspective while engendering action. My plea is that everyone should also examine organizational behaviors and outcomes through the prism of his or her beliefs. Doing so will undoubtedly yield results over time that one can be proud of having created the right way.

MILLENNIAL TAKEAWAY

Adam Braun

At one point a few years ago when we had built just a few schools, I wrote in my journal that if Pencils of Promise built 30 schools by the time I turned 30, I could die a happy man. Today we've opened more than 150. But here's the important part—I was wrong about being able to die a happy man. I still want to do so much more. As soon as something becomes possible, you start thinking of what you can do next. Each stage on which I gave a speech gave me the confidence to go bigger, each country I traveled to made me hungry to visit another, and no matter how late I stayed out at night, I always had an urge to watch the sunrise.

So as I stand on the frontier of a new decade, I now realize what my twenties taught me: There is no such thing as *best*. The finish line to living the perfect life doesn't exist. It's constantly in motion, just ahead of our grasp, moving forward at the same rate of acceleration as the expectations that will inevitably trail our accomplishments.

You will screw up, you will be celebrated, and you will feel like a loser and a winner all in the same day. And that will happen over and over. But the people who succeed are those who dust themselves off and keep going because they're not motivated by hitting their goals. They're motivated by getting to a place where they can set new goals that seem just as unreasonable as the ones before them once did.

Take a moment to grasp that fully—the most successful people are *not* motivated by reaching their goals. They're motivated by getting to a place where they can confidently and audaciously move the finish line farther into the distance.

So set incredibly ambitious goals. Chase them with fervor. And then move the finish line far off into the distance.

WHAT IS OUR PLAN?

Peter F. Drucker

- Should the mission be changed?
- What are our goals?

———

The self-assessment process leads to a plan that is a concise summation of the organization's purpose and future direction. The plan encompasses mission, vision, goals, objectives, action steps, a budget, and appraisal. [See Figure 5.1] Now comes the point to affirm or change the mission and set long-range goals. Remember, every mission statement has to reflect three things: opportunities, competence, and commitment. It answers the questions, *What is our purpose? Why do we do what we do? What, in the end, do we want to be remembered for?* The mission transcends today but guides

Figure 5.1 The parts of a plan

today, informs today. It provides the framework for setting goals and mobilizing the resources of the organization for getting the right things done.

The development and formal adoption of mission and goals are fundamental to effective governance of a nonprofit organization and are primary responsibilities of the board. Therefore, these strategic elements of the plan must be approved by the board.

To further the mission, there must be action today and specific aims for tomorrow. Yet planning is not masterminding the future. Any attempt to do so is foolish; the future is unpredictable. In the face of uncertainties, planning defines the particular place you *want* to be and how you intend to get there. Planning does not substitute facts for judgment, nor science for leadership. It recognizes the importance of analysis, courage, experience, intuition—even hunch. It is responsibility rather than technique.

GOALS ARE FEW, OVERARCHING, AND APPROVED BY THE BOARD

The most difficult challenge is to agree on the institution's goals—the fundamental long-range direction. Goals are overarching and should be few in number. If you have more than five goals, you have none. You're simply spreading yourself too thin. Goals make it absolutely clear where you will concentrate resources for results—the mark of an organization serious about success. Goals flow from mission, aim the organization where it must go, build on strength, address opportunity, and taken together, outline your desired future.

An option for the plan is a vision statement picturing a future when the organization's goals are achieved and its mission accomplished. The Drucker Foundation's vision is *A society that recognizes the social sector as the leading force in creating healthy communities and improving the quality of life.* I have worked with groups who became intensely motivated by these often-idealistic and poetic statements, whereas others say, "Let's not get carried away." If a vision statement—whether a sentence or a page—helps bring the plan to life, by all means include it.

Here is an example of the vision, mission, and goals for an art museum.

> **Vision:** A city where the world's diverse artistic heritage is prized and whose people seek out art to feed their mind and spirit.
> **Mission:** To bring art and people together.

Goal 1: To conserve the collections and inspire partnerships to seek and acquire exceptional objects.

Goal 2: To enable people to discover, enjoy, and understand art through popular and scholarly exhibitions, community education, and publications.

Goal 3: To significantly expand the museum's audience and strengthen its impact with new and traditional members.

Goal 4: To maintain state-of-the-art facilities, technologies, and operations.

Goal 5: To enhance long-term financial security.

Building around mission and long-term goals is the only way to integrate shorter-term interests. Then management can always ask, "Is an objective leading us toward our basic long-range goal, or is it going to sidetrack us, divert us, make us lose sight of our aims?" St. Augustine said, "One prays for miracles but works for results." Your plan leads you to work for results. It converts intentions into action.

OBJECTIVES ARE MEASURABLE, CONCRETE, AND THE RESPONSIBILITY OF MANAGEMENT

Objectives are the specific and measurable levels of achievement that move the organization toward its goals. The chief executive officer is responsible for development of objectives and action steps and detailed budgets that follow. The board must not act at the level of tactical planning, or it interferes with management's vital ability to be flexible in how goals are achieved. When developing and implementing a plan, the board is accountable for mission, goals, and the allocation of resources to results, and for appraising progress and achievement. Management is accountable for objectives, for action steps, for the supporting budget, as well as for demonstrating effective performance.

FIVE ELEMENTS OF EFFECTIVE PLANS

Abandonment: The first decision is whether to abandon what does not work, what has never worked—the things that have outlived their usefulness and their capacity to contribute. Ask of any program, system, or customer group, "If we were not committed to this today, would we go into it?" If the answer is no, say "How can we get out—fast?"

Concentration: Concentration is building on success, strengthening what *does* work. The best rule is to put your efforts into your successes. You will get maximum results. When you have strong performance is the very time to ask, "Can we set an even higher standard?" Concentration is vital, but it's also very risky. You must choose the right concentrations, or—to use a military term—you leave your flanks totally uncovered.

Innovation: You must also look for tomorrow's success, the true innovations, the diversity that stirs the imagination. What are the opportunities, the new conditions, the emerging issues? Do they fit you? Do you really believe in this? But you have to be careful. Before you go into something new, don't say, "This is how we do it." Say, "Let's find out what this requires. What does the customer value? What is the state of the art? How can we make a difference?" Finding answers to these questions is essential.

Risk taking: Planning always involves decisions on where to take the risks. Some risks you can afford to take—if something goes wrong, it is easily reversible with minor damage. And some decisions may carry great risk, but you cannot afford *not* to take it. You have to balance the short range with the long. If you are too conservative, you miss the opportunity. If you commit too much too fast, there may not be a long run to worry about. There is no formula for these risk-taking decisions. They are entrepreneurial and uncertain, but they must be made.

Analysis: Finally, in planning it is important to recognize when you do *not* know, when you are not yet sure whether to abandon, concentrate, go into something new, or take a particular risk. Then your objective is to conduct an analysis. Before making the final decision, you study a weak but essential performance area, a challenge on the horizon, the opportunity just beginning to take shape.

BUILD UNDERSTANDING AND OWNERSHIP

The plan begins with a mission. It ends with *action steps* and a *budget*. Action steps establish accountability for objectives—who will do what by when—and the budget commits the resources necessary to implement the plan. To build understanding and ownership for the plan, action steps are developed by the people who will carry them out. Everyone with a role should have the opportunity to give input. This looks incredibly slow. But when the plan is completed, the next day everyone understands it. More people in the organization want the new, are committed to it, are ready to act.

The Assessment Team will prepare the final plan for review by the board. Following presentation and discussion, the board chairman will request approval of the mission, goals, and supporting budget. The chairman may request adoption of a vision statement, if one has been developed, as part of the plan. As soon as approval is given, implementation begins.

NEVER REALLY BE SATISFIED

This is the last of the self-assessment questions, and your involvement as a participant soon draws to a close. Appraisal will be ongoing. The organization must monitor progress in achieving goals and meeting objectives, and above all, must measure results in changed lives. You must adjust the plan when conditions change, results are poor, there is a surprise success, or when the customer leads you to a place different from where you imagined.

True self-assessment is never finished. Leadership requires constant resharpening, refocusing, never really being satisfied. I encourage you especially to keep asking the question, *What do we want to be remembered for?* It is a question that induces you to renew yourself—and the organization—because it pushes you to see what you can become.[1]

WHAT IS OUR PLAN?

V. Kasturi Rangan

Planning is the process of translating the organization's strategic or mission goals into a set of actionable programs and tracing the path of how they would meet the goals of the organization. According to Peter F. Drucker, the organization's mission is a key element in its plan, along with vision, goals, objectives, action steps, a budget, and appraisal. He goes on to say that when prepared correctly, the mission statement will answer three questions: *What is our purpose? Why do we do what we do? What, in the end, do we want to be remembered for?*

Although Drucker focuses on the organizational aspect of these three questions, it is my observation that these questions apply equally well to *individual entrepreneurs*—particularly young people who have a passionate desire to change the world they live in for the better.

As a professor of marketing, it's not uncommon for students to excitedly bring me their ideas for new products that they are convinced will have a positive effect on the lives of thousands, if not millions, of people—particularly the poor and disenfranchised. They are uniformly convinced that their ideas have so much merit that they will of their own accord gain the momentum they need to become successful.

While many of these ideas may indeed be good ones, almost every young entrepreneur who brings them to me shares the same fundamental problem: He or she has no concrete plan for turning the good idea into reality.

Consider the example of an enthusiastic entrepreneur who recently brought me her idea for a sanitary pad produced from locally available plant materials that were freely available at no cost. "It will be affordable and widely available," she gushed, "enabling thousands of teenage girls to be at work or at school without having to miss any days in between." To her credit, she had a precise production cost estimate, as well as a price target. But when pushed on the question, "Who is the customer—the teenage girl, her mother, or her father—and who will pay?" she took a step back and started to ponder.

In my experience, young people are not short of ideas—in fact, they are brimming with them. But without a plan, they are just ideas. And it takes more than ideas to identify the real barriers to end user adoption, to construct a supply chain, to raise money, to launch a new product or service, to gain distribution, and to bring closure to the strategic goals. When I talk with my students about creating a plan to make their ideas real, I usually ask them to think in great depth about the answers to four specific questions:

1. What is the problem you are trying to solve, and for whom are you trying to solve it? The lack of availability of sanitary pads at an affordable price is a significant problem in developing countries, but there is more to the problem than initially meets the eye. Clearly, the young women themselves, those in the target audience, do not have the resources to undertake the purchase, so who will be the buyer on their behalf? What are the social and cultural attitudes toward this new product in

the household? What are the current prevailing practices? For an idea to be useful, it must be adapted to the realities on the ground. Can you solve the problem? Will it be of use to the end user? Will the buyer be motivated to buy?

2. *How will you complete the value chain?* Products don't just appear out of thin air; they must be designed, prototyped, tested, built, marketed, sold, distributed, and serviced after the sale. For even the simplest products, this value chain is complex. For example, this young entrepreneur had worked out quite an elaborate supply chain from a specific plant waste with excellent absorptive powers. But would the raw material still be available for free once someone had set up a commercial entity to convert it? Would locally manufactured products still have the same specifications and consistency as the prototypes worked out in a laboratory? Would the product be sold door-to-door or through retail outlets? The supporting logistics and the costs will obviously be different for the two different go-to-market options. Pricing has to not only consider affordability and value for the customer but also consider realistic supply chain costs. Otherwise the spreadsheet projections (which by the way are very easy to do these days because of software availability) can be made to look rosy without being realistic.

3. *What is your plan for launch?* Once the idea has been reasonably vetted, and the value chain more or less identified, then a business plan must be created with goals and benchmarks and with contingencies built in. Notice that I am not suggesting that an entrepreneur have the answers to all the questions regarding

the end user and the supply chain before diving in. It is good to know the alternate assumptions and alternate paths so that one can iterate and adjust if one path does not work as expected. To be effective, the plan must contain the following central elements:

- *A focus on a few operational goals*: Entrepreneurs do not like to write formal operating plans. They consider it a burden and a waste of time. Yet this is something that all funders will demand. But unlike large organizations that tend to write detailed plans with all aspects of marketing, selling, producing, and procuring, entrepreneurs—especially individual entrepreneurs—are better off writing a simpler plan that brings down a few key goals to an operational level. These operational goals should be simple enough to fit a on 3 × 5 note card rather than in a blue binder. When these few operational goals dovetail into each other, it should produce a financial statement. A profit and loss statement is less useful than a cash flow statement with growth projections and investment requirements. Whether the entrepreneur likes it or not, without such a financial analysis, no funder is likely to come up with significant investments to seed the business and grow it.

- *Steady but not dogmatic in direction*: "Planning is not masterminding the future. Any attempt to do so is foolish; the future is unpredictable," wrote Drucker in a previous edition of this self-assessment tool. That's why it is crucially important to keep an open mind regarding the several potential alternative ways of getting to the goal, even while staying steady regarding a chosen direction, until a crossover to a different path has been decided. Flexibility and a learning attitude have to be two important characteristics of an effective plan. Passion and ideas drive entrepreneurs. Managing uncertainty should be part of one's DNA, so when an inference about customers or costs goes awry, it means that the plan needs adjustment, not abandonment. That's why it is so important to have thought through alternate paths and assumptions earlier on, so one can make the adjustments based on the new data from the field and go back to the field with a revised approach.

- *Monitoring*: Monitoring is essential to better strategy. The main purpose of monitoring the execution is to understand the logic of the plan and its components and whether they are acting the way they were supposed to. Thus, if the purpose of a door-to-door campaign is to convince the mother of the value of the sanitary pad so that she will in turn influence her daughter to adopt and convince her husband to buy it, then it is crucial to monitor the quantity and quality of such house calls, before one looks at sales results. All the major components of a plan must be broken down into measurable chunks and be monitored. Entrepreneurs are notorious for not doing so. They look at aggregate results and go by their hunches as to what worked and what didn't, thus missing a huge opportunity to bring data and rationality to bear on their ideas and enthusiasm.

4. *What is your exit strategy?* By *exit strategy* I don't exclusively mean executing an initial public offering (IPO) or otherwise cashing out of the business. That may be a possibility, but when it comes to social enterprise, it means ensuring continuity of the solution to ensure the long-term sustainability of the idea itself. Going back to the example of the sanitary pad, although a business might make a go of directly selling the pads in a small market, chances are the idea will have much greater success if the business can partner with a nonprofit or a health care delivery agency that is on the ground in the developing country to take on responsibility for educating and distributing them to individuals. This would help ensure the long-term sustainability of both the idea and the social value itself. Scaling is perhaps the hardest thing to do, especially in social enterprise, because what works in one ecosystem might be inappropriate for another. Social entrepreneurs should carefully study all aspects of a successful model and scale only when they are able to replicate the critical elements. If not, getting appropriate partners to be part of the collaborative will need to be an integral part of the plan.

PLANNING FOR SUSTAINABILITY: THE STORY OF MI CASA

Juana Bordas

According to Peter F. Drucker, there are five elements of effective plans: abandonment, concentration, innovation, risk taking, and analysis. Although this may be the case, how do you know whether all the work you have put into the planning process has truly been effective?

In my experience, the best way for leaders to know they have done effective planning is to see their organizations stand the test of time. In 1976 I attended the organizing meeting for Mi Casa Resource Center for Women. I stayed 10 years—serving as president of the board, director of youth programs, and then executive director until 1986. Almost 40 years later, Mi Casa is Colorado's largest Hispanic-serving organization, and it is recognized nationally as a model for economic empowerment and self-sufficiency for Latinas.

What lessons about planning can be learned from a community-based nonprofit that survived and thrived the most tumultuous of economic and political times? How can Millennials who want to start entrepreneurial social ventures or their own businesses use these lessons to plan for and successfully sustain organizations today?

A Plan for Leadership

Mi Casa's organizing committee consisted of Head Start mothers and professional Hispanic women. Bringing together people whom by Mi Casa would serve and women with experience in organizations was crucial. The customer was at the organizing table. The professional women, like me, had grown up in similar circumstances and understood what was needed for Latinas to become successful. This made for an organization that was customer centered, a key element—and I believe a prerequisite—for successful long-term planning.

A Plan That Is Customer Centered and Results Oriented

It is easy to know your customers when they are sitting at the table in leadership roles. Yet Drucker cautions, "The danger is in acting on what you believe satisfies the customer...go to the customer." We designed a door-to-door survey to determine what low-income Hispanic women wanted. The results were not earthshaking: good jobs, high school completion, English proficiency, a supportive place to learn, and help for young Latinas with finishing school. These needs continue to be the core of Mi Casa's programs.

Success would also depend on garnering *supporting customers*—volunteers, funders, other organizations, and community leaders. Mi Casa built partnerships with corporations and foundations by focusing on numbers and results.

When I was director, a funder could be assured that by investing $1,800 in a program for a high-risk Latina youth to complete high school, Colorado would receive $200,000 in taxes over the young person's life. Eighty-five percent would complete high school, and more than half would go on to higher education. If funders were looking for a qualified workforce for the future, Mi Casa would deliver.

Today, Mi Casa carries on that tradition by incorporating programs into its planning process that meet the needs of today's employers: bilingual bank tellers, computer classes, health care, and customer service programs.

A Plan Based on a Mission for Changing Times

The most important driver for long-term planning is the mission. As Drucker notes, "The plan begins with a mission."

Mi Casa did not just have a mission—it also had women who were on a mission. In 1976, forging a Hispanic women's nonprofit corporation was groundbreaking and inspiring. Moreover, Mi Casa's logo—a house with the women's symbol inside—signified that as Latinas advanced, so would their families and communities. The mission was broad enough to engender a new one in 2008: to advance the economic success of *Latino families*.

Even though Mi Casa focused on Hispanics, the organization welcomed others. It was both culturally centered and inclusive. This is particularly pertinent for Millennials today: How do you build organizations that are inclusive of four generations that work side by side? How do you plan to serve our ever-growing diversity?

A Plan That Is Culturally Centered and Inclusive

Organizations that serve distinct populations must be responsive to the special needs of their customers. Mi Casa was a cultural oasis where Hispanic women could gain confidence and learn skills needed to be successful in the dominant culture.

The first house rented in the neighborhood had a sign on the door saying *Bienvenido to Mi Casa,* reflecting Latino values of generosity, sharing, and inclusiveness. The organization's success has rested on that open-door policy. Mi Casa was one of the first Hispanic organizations to diversify its board of directors. These community influencials became advocates for success. Inclusion takes careful planning, outreach, relationship building, and a welcoming spirit!

A Plan Informed by Learning That Ensures Future Success

Drucker cautions organizations not to subordinate the mission for money. In the 1980s, foundations urged nonprofits to launch businesses to generate funds. After a careful analysis of market needs, of the skills our women had, and of finding start-up money and partners, Mi Casa launched A Woman's Touch—a cleaning service where participants could earn 30 percent more than they could from similar jobs in the marketplace. Within a year, women left to start their own cleaning services. Gone was the original plan to generate operating revenue from this venture. But we knew how to run a business.

Often mistakes are our biggest teachers. Latinas today are the fastest-growing small-business sector. In 1988, Mi Casa launched its business center to assist Latinas and other aspiring entrepreneurs in developing businesses. In 2013, 80 new businesses were launched, generating $7.5 million in revenues.

A Plan That Sustains

Although decades of planning, experience, and learning have spurred new programs, Mi Casa's core mission remains. We learned that effective planning for the long term requires the following key elements:

- The mission must have deep meaning yet be adaptable to changing conditions—it is most powerful when it comes from the people it serves
- Always customer focused but results oriented
- Led by a community of leaders (staff, board, customers, and community partners) where ownership and accountability is distributed—engendering continuity and success
- A strong focus on program goals and monitoring of customers served, cost, and satisfaction—ensuring accountability
- Nurturing an inclusive environment while providing culturally centered services
- Remaining flexible and always learning—a so-called mistake can become a great asset

Historical note: The emerging Hispanic influence is a recent historical phenomenon buoyed by the civil rights movement in the 1960s and by the founding of many organizations in the 1970s and 1980s. Mi Casa's founding in 1976 therefore makes it one of the first Hispanic organizations to focus on serving women.

MILLENNIAL TAKEAWAY

Caroline Ghosn

As a leader, the most important thing you can do is articulate a vision. Doing so convenes people smarter, more experienced, and better than you in every way—with gathering speed—to move your organization collectively toward that distant horizon. You cannot translate a vision without a clear plan, for that is the tangible matter that people can wrap their arms around once you have successfully inspired them to join forces with you. The clearer your plan, the lesser the loss factor between the people you inspire and those who decide to commit, and the lesser the loss factor between the people who decide to commit and the actions they perform in moving toward your shared goal. Keep that pipeline of vision translation leak-free—your most powerful sealant is your plan.

Significant data show that companies founded and driven by Millennials—and specifically, Millennial females, who index highest—have the highest chance of success. That isn't a coincidence. Millennials are willing to create tenacious plans as architectures for where they're going but then iterate and experiment within the confines of those plans to learn as they go. When you talk about a plan, you're talking about something that is alive and that changes when necessary—not a dead document that is just filed away. A plan becomes the shared basis for brain play, the sandbox in which you can experiment with the most brilliant minds in your organization and ensure you're visualizing the same end, as well as a thermometer that measures the heat of the sand.

When you interview Millennials, many of them say things such as, "I want to create something that changes the world," "I want to affect the environment," or "I want to affect the state of women in the world through education." There is no dearth of problems in need of audacious solutions, many of which are set to a stubbornly ticking clock. We Millennials have been birthed in that fire and it requires moving *fast*. But moving fast doesn't mean moving without a direction. Quite the opposite—the faster you go, the more small deltas from the straight line you intended to follow create larger diversions, slowed impact, and cost accumulations. Having a plan and gathering the data that help you assess whether you need to make small iterations inside of that plan keep you focused.

In some cases, big iterations are needed. In others, a plan might take you to a point where you realize the hypothesis that it was built on no longer works moving forward. That's a successful plan. Think like a scientist: If you arrive at a point where your hypothesis is found to be wrong, good. You just saved time, and you've learned something valuable. You have to have experimental structure, boundaries, and edges that define success and failure, and those are what make up a plan.

Luck comes to those who are prepared, as the old adage goes, and that preparation is the only reliable tool you have in your arsenal as a visionary leader to potentially stack the deck in your favor. A plan measures the wins that you'll encounter and mitigates the losses by creating milestones that signal, "Wrong way! Turn around!" before doing so becomes too expensive. A well-crafted plan creates a common language around which people in an organization can all move together in that direction.

TRANSFORMATIONAL LEADERSHIP

Frances Hesselbein

In a world where the rules are constantly changing, millions of people in every sector of the economy are wrestling with the new demands of leadership. I hear leaders and managers everywhere discussing the same fundamental challenge: the journey to transformation, moving from where we are to where we want to be in the tenuous future that lies before us. Around the world—in universities, the community of faith, corporations, government, and the burgeoning social sector—leaders are working to shape the transformation of their institutions.

A few years ago, I ventured to China with a team of four thought leaders to deliver a series of seminars at the invitation of the Bright China Management Institute. As we talked with our Chinese colleagues, we used the same language to describe the power of mission that we use when we work with the Salvation Army, the U.S. Army, Chevron, or the American Institute of Architects: vision, mission, goals. The actual words are different in every language, but the power of those words is universal. And with a common language, people in every sector, in every culture, can have dialogues of great meaning that help transform organizations.

In sharing experiences across the public, private, and social sectors, I have found that organizations usually pass eight milestones to reach their destination: an inspired, relevant, viable, effective organization. These milestones are as relevant to a small community group or the Girl Scouts as they are to a large business or government agency.

1. *Scan the environment.* Through reading, surveys, interviews, and so on, we identify the major trends likely to affect the organization. The essence of strategy is to define the implications of those trends. Sometimes we can catch a straw in the wind and have a responsive program or project ready as the trend emerges—not after. This assessment of emerging trends and implications, supplemented by internal data, provides essential background for planning change—and offers a better basis for action than our own preconceptions. Flying on assumptions can be fatal. Enstitute, a nonprofit founded by Kane Sarhan and Shaila Ittycheria, works to address both the growing cost of higher education as well as the current youth unemployment crisis by providing young adults with

one-year, full-time, apprenticeships at high-growth startups, small businesses, and corporations around the country to prepare them for the workforce and accelerate their career trajectory. Enstitute makes the connection between fellows in need and entrepreneurs and executives willing to mentor those fellows while working together toward a shared goal. After recently launching a second program in Washington, DC (Enstitute began in New York City) Kane and Shaila announced that their program will expand to St. Louis, which came to mind after a recent *Forbes* article cited St. Louis as having some of the highest startup growth in America. This unique possibility held the opportunity to work in a city on the rise. Kane and Shaila are always looking to the future: they plan to have 500 fellows by next year.

2. *Revisit the mission.* At the Frances Hesselbein Leadership Institute, we review our mission every three years and refine it if necessary. The foundation is now 25 years old, and we've revisited and refined our mission a number of times—honing our focus, practicing planned abandonment, and even renaming our foundation—not because we couldn't get it right the first time, with Peter F. Drucker in the room, but when Peter passed, his name belonged to his family.

   The mission statement simply describes why we do what we do, our reason for being—our purpose. Knowing that management is a tool, not an end, we manage not for the sake of managing in its own right, but for the mission. And one's mission does not define how one operates, but simply why. It must be clear, powerful, compelling, and to the point.

When we revisit the mission, we ask ourselves the first three of the five most important questions that Drucker helped organizations answer:

- What is our mission?
- Who is our customer?
- What does the customer value?

When we answer these, we are well on our way to managing for the mission.

3. *Ban the hierarchy.* Transformation requires moving people out of their old organizational boxes into flexible, fluid management systems. We cannot continue to put people into little squares on a structure chart. Psychologically it boxes them in. We prefer circles—concentric circles of functions and positions in a staffing design that looks almost organic. Job rotation becomes an enriching reality. People move in circular ways—learning new skills, expanding positions—circular management. We need to ban a hierarchy not suited to today's knowledge workers, who carry their toolkits in their heads.

4. *Challenge the gospel.* There should be no sacred cows as we challenge every policy, practice, procedure, and assumption. In transforming themselves, organizations must practice planned abandonment—discarding programs, policies, and practices that work today but will have little relevance to the future and to the organization we are building to meet that future.

5. *Employ the power of language.* Leaders must beam a few clear, consistent messages over and over. They must lead by voice, communicating with all their customers, and all

their constituents, a few powerful messages that connect and illuminate. Airbnb is a global community marketplace that connects travelers seeking authentic, high-quality accommodations with hosts who offer unique places to stay. When founders Nathan Blecharczyk, Brian Chesky, and Joe Gebbia asked themselves "What is our mission?" all signs pointed to a sense of "belonging." What makes our global community relevant for Airbnb customers is that for the very first time, anyone can belong anywhere. That is the idea at the core of their company: belonging. Such powerful aspirations—and the language to go with them—are essential to guide an organization into transformation.

6. *Disperse leadership across the organization.* Every organization must have not one but many leaders. Some speak of empowerment, others of sharing the tasks of leadership. I think of it as dispersing leadership—with leaders developing and performing across every level of the organization. Leadership is a responsibility all members of the organization share, and it is circular.

7. *Lead from the front; don't push from the rear.* The leader of the future does not sit on the fence, waiting to see which way the wind is blowing. The leader articulates clear positions on issues affecting the organization and is the embodiment of the enterprise, its mission, its values, and its principles. Leaders model desired behaviors, they never break a promise, and they know that leadership is a matter of how to be, not how to do.

8. *Assess performance.* Self-assessment is essential to progress. From the beginning of the change process, we are clear about

mission, goals, and objectives. Well-defined action steps and a plan for measuring results are essential to planning any organizational change. We then can embark upon the journey with goals and measures in place. At the end of the process, the most exuberant phase of the journey, we evaluate our performance and celebrate the transformation. We do this by asking the next two of Drucker's five critical questions discussed earlier:

- What are our results?
- What is our plan?

Across the globe, for leaders aware of the tenuous times ahead, the journey to transformation is a journey into the future. These leaders are taking today's organization and transforming it into tomorrow's productive, high-performance enterprise. Although the milestones on the journey are known, the destinations are uncharted, and for each organization the destination will be determined not only by the curve of the road ahead but also by the quality of the mission and the leadership it inspires.

MILLENNIAL TAKEAWAY

Lauren Maillian Bias

Becoming a single parent before the age of 30 made me refine and hone what I look for in a life partner. The same characteristics that are most important to me today in a personal relationship are the same characteristics that are most important to me in business relationships. Considering the *quality* of a leader has helped me become a better businessperson at the same time.

For Millennials, more than any previous generation, our professional success and our personal success are interdependent. That's why so many of the qualities and characteristics that we look for in others in our personal life can be applied to our professional life.

Organizations aren't hiring candidates only for the skills listed on their resume. Someone might be highly skilled but also unfocused, unsure of a solid moral compass, untrustworthy, and unreliable.

Every day of the week, employers will choose to hire, collaborate, or partner with someone they can trust, someone reliable, someone who is intelligent and adaptive, who can roll with the punches, and who is willing and able to learn whatever it is he or she needs to know to effectively do the job.

This was my own story for transforming my life and my career. I was tapped to help start up Gen Y Capital Partners in the early stage venture world—not because I was an amazing investor, but because I was a very good judge of character, because I had a very analytical mind regarding investment opportunities, and because people knew that I was fully committed to doing whatever I said I was going to do and to learning whatever I needed to know to succeed as an early stage investor.

By carefully considering the characteristics and qualities that are most important to you in your personal life, you can undergo a transformation in your business life. As Frances Hesselbein notes, "in the end it is the quality and character of the leader that determines results."

THE SELF-ASSESSMENT PROCESS

Peter F. Drucker

The *Self-Assessment Tool* was intentionally developed as a flexible resource. How you use this book will depend on your setting and the particular purpose for which self-assessment is being undertaken. The Workbook has not arrived on your doorstep on its own. It is in your hands because you have an interest in it or an Assessment Team, an instructor, a manager, or leader has thought through a self-assessment process design, identified a role for you, and asked you to participate. It is the responsibility of that team or individual to explain the purpose for self-assessment and to orient you to specific time and task expectations.

The self-assessment process calls for broad participation to ensure understanding, ownership, and readiness to act. Certain adaptations of the self-assessment process are discrete and may be completed within a matter of weeks. Comprehensive self-assessment for an organization takes place in three phases over a number of months. A detailed Process Guide shows those leading self-assessment how to properly organize and direct it.

This Workbook has a twofold purpose: *(1) to guide your individual thinking and (2) to prepare you and others for productive discussion and decision making.* To make the most of what is offered here, you will do three things:

1. Thoroughly review the information that is provided on your organization, its customers, trends in its operating environment, and other self-assessment materials or reports.
2. Sit down with this Workbook and, in one or more sessions, take the necessary time to read it through and give a thoughtful response to the important questions it asks.
3. Actively participate in a retreat, group discussions, a one-to-one depth interview, or in other self-assessment meetings.

My final word on how to use this book: Please don't rush through it at the last minute. The five questions appear simple, but they are not. Give them time to sink in; wrestle over them. Properly carried through, self-assessment develops skill, competence, and commitment. Active and attentive participation is an opportunity to enhance your vision and *to shape the future.*[1]

SUGGESTED QUESTIONS TO EXPLORE*

The most important aspect of the *Self-Assessment Tool* is the questions it poses. Answers are important; you need answers because you need action. But the most important thing is to ask these questions.

—PETER F. DRUCKER*

QUESTION 1: WHAT IS OUR MISSION?

As you work through the overarching question "What is our mission?" consider the following additional questions—they may help you find the answers you seek:

What Are We Trying to Achieve?*

- What is your organization's current understanding of the organization's mission?*
- What is your organization's reason for being?*
- Why do you do what you do?*
- For what, in the end, do you want to be remembered?*

What Are the Significant External or Internal Challenges, Opportunities, and Issues?

- What significant challenges is the organization facing—changing demographics, legislation or regulations, emerging technologies, and competition?
- What significant opportunities are presenting themselves—partnerships and collaborations, leading-edge practices or approaches, social or cultural trends?
- What are the emerging critical issues for the organization—need for multilingual employees, community-based issues, market share, rising cost of health care, changing distribution channels?

Does Our Mission Need to Be Revisited?*

- Does the mission statement need to be redefined? If not, why not? If yes, why is that?*

- In what ways, if any, would you rewrite or refocus the mission statement for your organization?*
- What would be the major benefits of a new mission? Why do you say that?*
- What problems, if any, would you be likely to encounter with the new mission? Among whom? Why is that? What steps, if any, may need to be taken to effect this change?*

QUESTION 2: WHO IS OUR CUSTOMER?

As you work through the overarching question "Who is our customer?" consider the following additional questions—they may help you find the answers you seek:

Who Are Our Customers?

- Create a list of those who use the organization's products or services? For nonprofits, from that list identify who is the primary customer—the people whose lives are changed through the organization's work. For businesses, from the list identify who the primary customer is currently and determine if that customer can and will sustain the organization based on demographic potential and so on? For public institutions, often the primary customer is determined through legislation or by the government authority establishing the organization.
- Create a list of supporting customers—the volunteers, members, partners, funders, referral sources, employees, and

others—both inside and outside the organization who must be satisfied.

- What value do we provide each of these customers?*
- Do our strengths, our competencies, and resources match the needs of these customers? If yes, in what way? If not, why not?*

Have Our Customers Changed?*

- In what ways, if any, have your customers changed? Think in terms of . . .*
  - Demographics? (age, sex, race, ethnicity)*
  - Primary needs? (training, shelter, day care, and so on)*
  - Number? (greater, fewer)*
  - Physical and psychological well-being? (such as drug dependence, family dysfunction)*
  - Other ways? (for example, location, workplace)*
- What are the implications of these changes for your organization?*

Should We Add or Delete Some Customers?*

- What *other groups* of customers, if any, *should the organization be serving?* Why is that?*
- What special competencies does the organization have to benefit them?*
- What *groups of current customers*, if any, *should the organization no longer serve?**

- Why is that? (Their needs have changed? Your resources are too limited? Other organizations are more effective? Their needs do not fit your organization's mission? Its competencies?)*

QUESTION 3: WHAT DOES THE CUSTOMER VALUE?

As you work through the overarching question "What does the customer value?" consider the following additional questions—they may help you find the answers you seek:

What Do Our Customers Value?*

- Think about value in terms of what your organization does that fills a specific need, provides satisfaction, or offers a benefit to your primary customers that they do not receive from another source. For each group of primary customers . . . briefly describe what each values about your organization.*
- Think about value in terms of what your organization does that fills a specific need, provides satisfaction, or offers a benefit to your secondary customers that they do not receive from another source. For each group of supporting customers . . . briefly describe what each values about your organization.*
- What are our customers' long-term aspirations, and what is our capacity and competency to deliver on those aspirations?

- How well does your organization provide what each of your customers considers value?*
- How can the knowledge you have about what your customers consider value be used to make decisions in areas like those listed?*
  - Products or services
  - Recruitment
  - Training
  - Innovation
  - Fund development
  - Marketing
  - Other
- What resources—internal and external—can you use to determine your customers' level of satisfaction? For example, do you need to conduct a survey of current customers as well as those who no longer use your service?*
- What do our *supporting* customers consider value?*
- If they are donors, do they value recognition or a sense that their contribution is helping solve a community problem?
- If they are volunteers, do they give of their time because they seek to learn new skills, make new friends, feel that they are helping change lives?
- If they are related to the primary customer, do we know what their expectations are, as related to their family member?
- If they are distributors or members of the supply chain for our product or service, what are their needs and constraints related to their mission, profitability, and goals?

QUESTION 4: WHAT ARE OUR RESULTS?

As you work through the overarching question "What are our results?" consider the following additional questions—they may help you find the answers you seek:

How Do We Define Results for Our Organization?*

- Having thought through the first three Drucker questions on Mission, Customers, and Value . . . would you define "results" any differently? Why or why not?*
- How would you define results in the future?

To What Extent Have We Achieved These Results?*

- Considering your responses [to the questions in the previous section], to what extent has your organization achieved these results?*
- What are the major activities or programs that have helped (or hindered) the achievement of these results?*
- How will you measure results in the future, both qualitatively and quantitatively?

How Well Are We Using Our Resources?*

- How well is your organization using its human resources—its volunteers, board, staff, and so on? How do you know that? What *should* the organization be doing?*

- How well is your organization using its financial resources—such as its money, buildings, investments, gifts? How do you know that? What *should* the organization be doing?*
- How effectively are we attending to the value and positioning of our brand and our brand promise?
- What have been the results of your organization's efforts to attract and keep donors? Why is that?*
- How does the organization define and share its results with the donors? In what ways, if any, should it change its procedures? Why or why not?*
- Are other, similar organizations doing a better job of using their human and financial resources? Of attracting and satisfying donors? Of using their board? If yes, why is that? What can you learn from them?*

QUESTION 5: WHAT IS OUR PLAN?

As you work through the overarching question "What is our plan?" consider the following additional questions—they may help you find the answers you seek:

What Have We Learned, and What Do We Recommend?*

- List the most important lessons and summarize the actions they suggest.*
- Think about information that will help not only in the area for which you have responsibility but also in planning for the future direction and activities of the organization.*

Where Should We Focus Our Efforts?*

- List those areas where you believe *your group or area of responsibility* should be focused. Briefly state your reasons and how each one fits the mission.*
- Given what you have learned, list those areas where you believe *your organization* should be focused. Next, briefly state your reasons and how each one fits the mission.*

What, If Anything, Should We Do Differently?*

- Are there programs, activities, or customer needs that the organization should add?*
- Abandon?*
- Refer to other organizations, that is, "outsource" if it is unable to handle them effectively or efficiently in-house?*
- Why is that?*

What Is Our Plan to Achieve Results for the Organization?*

- What are the goals that will enable us to achieve the desired results?
- For nonprofits, what are the goals (fundamental aims) that will change lives and help us further the mission?
- What are the measurable objectives that will enable us to achieve our goals?

- What are the measurable action steps that will enable us to achieve our objectives?
- What are the budget implications of the resources required to achieve these goals, objectives, and action steps?
- What are the target dates for completion?
- Who will be responsible and accountable for achieving each goal, objective, and action step?
- What staffing will be needed to support this plan?
- How do we evaluate and measure the desired results?

What Is My Plan to Achieve Results for My Group or Responsibility Area?*

- Make a list of action items you have the authority to enact as well as those recommendations that need to be approved by appropriate board and staff teams.*
- Then establish a target date for approval and implementation.*
- Identify staff support needed.*

NOTES

FOREWORD

1. Peter F. Drucker, *The Five Most Important Questions You Will Ever Ask About Your Nonprofit Organization* (San Francisco: Jossey-Bass, 1993).

INTRODUCTION

1. Barnes & Noble College collaborated with Why Millennials Matter for a national study on the college student's mind-set related to career motivators, influences, and skills for success, www.bncollege.com/news/understanding-the-millennial-mindset.

WHY SELF ASSESSMENT?

1. Peter F. Drucker, *The Five Most Important Questions You Will Ever Ask About Your Nonprofit Organization* (San Francisco: Jossey-Bass, 1993), 2.

2. Gary J. Stern, *The Drucker Foundation Self-Assessment Tool: Process Guide,* rev. ed. (San Francisco: Jossey-Bass, 1999), 4.

3. Drucker, *Five Most Important Questions,* 3.

4. Stern, *Drucker Foundation Self-Assessment Tool,* 4.

5. Ibid.

6. Peter F. Drucker, *The Drucker Foundation Self-Assessment Tool: Participant Workbook,* rev. ed. (San Francisco: Jossey-Bass, 1999), 5.

7. Ibid., 6.

8. Ibid.

QUESTION 1: WHAT IS OUR MISSION?

1. Peter F. Drucker, *The Drucker Foundation Self-Assessment Tool: Participant Workbook,* rev. ed. (San Francisco: Jossey-Bass, 1999), 14–16.

QUESTION 2: WHO IS OUR CUSTOMER?

1. Peter F. Drucker, *The Drucker Foundation Self-Assessment Tool: Participant Workbook,* rev. ed. (San Francisco: Jossey-Bass, 1999), 22–24.

QUESTION 3: WHAT DOES THE CUSTOMER VALUE?

1. Peter F. Drucker, *The Drucker Foundation Self-Assessment Tool: Participant Workbook,* rev. ed. (San Francisco: Jossey-Bass, 1999), 32–34.

QUESTION 4: WHAT ARE OUR RESULTS?

1. Peter F. Drucker, *The Drucker Foundation Self-Assessment Tool: Participant Workbook*, rev. ed. (San Francisco: Jossey-Bass, 1999), 40–44.

2. George, Bill, *True North: Discover Your Authentic Leadership*, with Peter Sims (San Francisco: Jossey-Bass, 2007).

3. Headquarters, Department of the Army, *Army Leadership: ADRP 6–22* (Washington, DC: Training and Doctrine Command, 2011), 4–1.

QUESTION 5: WHAT IS OUR PLAN?

1. Peter F. Drucker, *The Drucker Foundation Self-Assessment Tool: Participant Workbook*, rev. ed. (San Francisco: Jossey-Bass, 1999), 52–56.

THE SELF-ASSESSMENT PROCESS

1. Peter F. Drucker, *The Drucker Foundation Self-Assessment Tool: Participant Workbook*, rev. ed. (San Francisco: Jossey-Bass, 1999), 7–8.

SUGGESTED QUESTIONS TO EXPLORE

Where indicated with an asterisk, the text is from Peter F. Drucker, *The Five Most Important Questions You Will Ever Ask about Your Nonprofit Organization* (San Francisco: Jossey-Bass, 1993). The text not attributed to Drucker in the form of an asterisk was contributed by trainers Maria Carpenter Ort and Tamara Woodbury—who have worked extensively with Drucker's *The Five Most Important Questions You Will Ever Ask about Your Nonprofit Organization*—along with project editor Peter Economy to address common situations not covered in Drucker's original text.

DEFINITIONS OF TERMS

Action steps: Detailed plans and activities directed toward meeting an organization's objectives.

Appraisal: Process for monitoring progress in meeting objectives and achieving results; point at which the plans for meeting objectives may be modified, based on experience or changed conditions.

Budget: The commitment of resources necessary to implement plans—the financial expression of a particular plan of work.

Customers: Those who must be satisfied in order for the organization to achieve results. The *primary customer* is the person whose life is changed through the organization's work. *Supporting customers* are volunteers, members, partners, funders, referral sources, employees, and others who must be satisfied.

Customer value: That which satisfies customers' *needs* (physical and psychological well-being), *wants* (where, when, and how service is provided), and *aspirations* (desired long-term results).

Depth interviews: One-on-one interviews used to highlight the insights of a select group of individuals inside the organization. Interview findings provide a touchstone for group discussions and decision making.

Goals: A set of three to five aims that set the organization's fundamental, long-range direction.

Mission: Why you do what you do; the organization's reason for being, its purpose. Says what, in the end, you want to be remembered for.

Objectives: Specific and measurable levels of achievement.

Plan: Your proposed approach to achieving the organization's goals, objectives, and action steps. To be effective, plans must contain firm target dates for completion; specific individuals who will be responsible and accountable for achievement and completion of goals, objectives, and action steps; and necessary human (people) and financial (money) resources.

Results: The organization's bottom line. Defined in *changed lives*— people's behavior, circumstances, health, hopes, competence, or capacity. Results are always *outside* the organization.

Vision: A picture of the organization's desired future.

NOTE

Except for the entry for *Plan,* the preceding text is from Peter F. Drucker, *The Drucker Foundation Self-Assessment Tool: Participant Workbook,* rev. ed. (San Francisco: Jossey-Bass, 1999), 9–10.

ADDITIONAL RESOURCES

- The Drucker Institute: www.druckerinstitute.com
- The Frances Hesselbein Leadership Institute: www.hesselbein institute.org
- *Leader to Leader* journal: www.leadertoleaderjournal.com
- Hesselbein Global Academy for Student Leadership and Civic Engagement: www.hesselbein.pitt.edu
- Frances Hesselbein Student Leadership Program: http://bit.ly /hesselbein
- Why Millennials Matter (Joan Snyder Kuhl): www.why millennialsmatter.com
- Col. Bernard Banks, HBR Blog Network: http://blogs.hbr.org /col-bernard-banks
- Juana Bordas: www.juanabordas.com
- Pencils of Promise (Adam Braun): www.pencilsofpromise.org
- Levo League (Caroline Ghosn): www.levo.com
- Marshall Goldsmith's blog: www.marshallgoldsmithfeed forward.com/marshallgoldsmithblog

- Nadira Hira's blog: www.nadirahira.com/blog
- Philip Kotler, *Harvard Business Review*: http://hbr.org/authors /kotler
- The Leadership Challenge (Jim Kouzes): www.leadership challenge.com
- Raghu Krishnamoorthy, HBR Blog Network: http://blogs.hbr .org/raghu-krishnamoorthy
- Raghu Krishnamoorthy, LinkedIn Blog: https://www.linkedin .com/today/author/26132621

ABOUT THE CONTRIBUTORS

Colonel Bernard Banks is the head of the Department of Behavioral Sciences & Leadership at the United States Military Academy, West Point. His numerous tactical command and staff positions have included assignments in the continental United States, the Republic of Korea, and the Middle East. Col. Banks has earned numerous awards and decorations, including the Bronze Star Medal and the Department of the Army's General Douglas MacArthur Leadership Award. He also holds a PhD in social-organizational psychology from Columbia University. Visit the United States Military Academy website at www.usma.edu.

Lauren Maillian Bias is the founder and chief executive officer (CEO) of LMB Group, a strategic marketing and branding consultancy where she brings her firsthand knowledge of, expertise in, and passion for marketing to her clients. She is also the founding partner for Gen Y Capital, an early stage venture firm. Before LMB Group, she was the proprietor, creator, and chief operating officer (COO) of Sugarleaf Vineyards, the only African American owned and operated winery in Virginia. She is author of the book *The Path Redefined: Getting to the Top on Your Own Terms*. Visit her website at www.laurenmbias.com.

Juana Bordas is president of Mestiza Leadership International and founding president/CEO of the National Hispana Leadership Institute. She served as a trustee of the Greenleaf Center for Servant Leadership and the International Leadership Association. She was the first Latina faculty at the Center for Creative Leadership. Bordas is the author of *Salsa, Soul, and Spirit—Leadership for a Multicultural Age*, which won the 2008 International Latino Book Award for leadership, and *The Power of Latino Leadership*, which was awarded the 2014 Nautilus Award for best multicultural book and the 2014 International Latino Book Award for leadership. Visit her website at www.mestizaleadership.com.

Adam Braun is a *New York Times* best-selling author and the founder of Pencils of Promise, an award-winning organization that has broken ground on more than 300 schools around the world. In recent years he has been named to the *Forbes* 30 Under 30 list, named to *Wired* magazine's 50 People Who Are Changing the World, and selected as one of the World Economic Forum's first 10 Global Shapers. He has also been a featured speaker at the White House, United Nations, and Clinton Global Initiative. He is author of the book *The Promise of a Pencil: How an Ordinary Person Can Create Extraordinary Change*. Visit his website at www.adambraun.com.

Jim Collins is one of the greatest thought leaders of his generation. He is a student and teacher of enduring great companies—how they grow, how they attain superior performance, and how good companies can become great companies. He is the author of such business classics as *Good to Great, Built to Last,* and *Great by Choice,* and the monograph *Good to Great and the Social Sectors.* Visit his website at www.jimcollins.com.

Caroline Ghosn is the cofounder and CEO of Levo League, a company that's using technology to mentor and arm its members with the tools needed to build excellence—to develop their talent, make connections, and learn from each other. Launched in 2012 with offices in New York and San Francisco, Levo has engaged more than 9 million professionals and become the largest and fastest-growing Generation Y movement in the workplace. Ghosn was recently named by *Fast Company* as one of the most creative people in business and by *Mashable* as a female founder every entrepreneur should know. Visit the Levo League website at www.levo.com.

Kelly Goldsmith joined the marketing faculty at the Kellogg School of Management in 2009 and was named a Donald P. Jacobs Scholar. Dr. Goldsmith's research focuses on consumer decision making, specifically examining how consumers' active goals and mind-sets affect their choices. Before joining Kellogg, Dr. Goldsmith obtained her PhD, MPhil and MA from Yale University. Visit the Kellogg School website at www.kellogg.northwestern.edu.

Marshall Goldsmith is a world authority in helping successful leaders achieve positive, lasting change in behavior: for themselves, their people, and their teams, and he was recognized in 2013 as one of the top 10 most influential business thinkers in the world, and the top-ranked executive coach, by Thinkers50. He is the million-copy-selling author or editor of 34 books, including the *New York Times* and *Wall Street Journal* best sellers *MOJO* and *What Got You Here Won't Get You There*—a *Wall Street Journal* number one business book and winner of the Harold Longman Award for Business Book of the Year. His books have been translated into 30 languages and have become best sellers in 12 countries. Visit his website at www.marshallgoldsmithlibrary.com.

Frances Hesselbein is the founding president of the Frances Hesselbein Leadership Institute, formerly the Peter F. Drucker Foundation for Nonprofit Management. She served as CEO of the Girl Scouts of the USA and was awarded the Presidential Medal of Freedom by President Bill Clinton. She is the author of *My Life in Leadership: The Journey and Lessons Learned Along the Way, Hesselbein on Leadership,* and *More Hesselbein on Leadership;* coeditor of numerous other books, including *Be, Know, Do;* and the editor in chief of the award-winning journal *Leader to Leader.* Visit the Institute's website at www.HesselbeinInstitute.org.

Nadira Hira is an award-winning writer, editor, speaker, television personality, all-around raconteur, and curator of great conversations. A member of *Cosmopolitan* magazine's Millennial Advisory Board, Hira is the author of the forthcoming *Misled: How a Generation of Leaders Lost the Faith (And Just What You'll Need to Get It Back).* Learn more about her work at www.nadirahira.com.

Philip Kotler is the S. C. Johnson & Son Distinguished Professor of International Marketing at the Northwestern University Kellogg Graduate School of Management in Chicago and the coauthor with Nancy Lee of the book *Corporate Social Responsibility: Doing the Most Good for Your Company and Cause*. In addition, Dr. Kotler has published more than 100 articles in leading journals, including the *Harvard Business Review*, *Sloan Management Review*, *Business Horizons*, *California Management Review*, and the *Journal of Marketing*. Visit the Kotler Marketing Group website at www.kotlermarketing.com.

Jim Kouzes is the coauthor with Barry Posner of the award-winning and best-selling book *The Leadership Challenge*, with more than 1 million copies sold. He is also an executive fellow at the Center for Innovation and Entrepreneurship, Leavey School of Business, Santa Clara University. In 2010, Kouzes received the Thought Leadership Award from the Instructional Systems Association, the most prestigious award given by the trade association of training and development industry providers. Visit Kouzes and Posner's website at www.leadershipchallenge.com/home.aspx.

Raghu Krishnamoorthy is responsible for General Electric's (GE) global talent pipeline, learning and development, and the Crotonville leadership development organization throughout the world. From 2009 to 2013, he was vice president, human resources, for GE Aviation, a $20 billion business. Before this, he was the human resources leader for GE Corporate's Commercial and Communications organization, responsible for enhancing the company's global commercial capabilities; he was also a member of GE's commercial council. Visit the GE website at www.ge.com.

Joan Snyder Kuhl has more than 13 years of corporate management experience working in the roles of sales, marketing, organizational effectiveness, training, and development at Eli Lilly and Forest Laboratories and Actavis, Inc. After a decade as a campus speaker, mentor, and coach to thousands of Millennials from around the world, Kuhl launched Why Millennials Matter. Why Millennials Matter is a Generation Y speaking, research, and consulting company based in New York City that focuses on raising employers' awareness about the value of investing in their younger workforce and the Millennial consumer segment. She is an international speaker, author, and board member of the Frances Hesselbein Leadership Institute and the *Cosmopolitan* magazine Millennial Advisory Board. Visit her website at www.whymillennialsmatter.com.

Kass Lazerow is a serial entrepreneur whose last company, Buddy Media, was acquired by Salesforce.com for $745 million. Before Buddy Media, Lazerow founded GOLF.com, which was sold to Time Inc. in 2006. At GOLF.com, she served as cofounder, president, and chief operating officer, where she helped take the company from an idea to a multimillion-dollar consumer Internet company. Lazerow is an active investor in digital media companies through Lazerow Ventures, an investment fund that has invested in more than 40 technology companies, including Facebook, Tumblr, BuzzFeed, *Mashable,* Domo, Rebel Mouse, and Namely. Visit her personal website at www.lazerow.com.

Mike Lazerow is a serial entrepreneur whose last company, Buddy Media, was acquired by Salesforce.com for $745 million. He is widely recognized as one of the most innovative leaders in digital media and marketing. His byline has appeared in *Fortune, Advertising Age,* Dow Jones' *AllThingsD, Fast Company,* and *Inc.,* among other publications, and he is a frequent guest on CNN, CNBC,

Bloomberg, the BBC, and other broadcast outlets. Lazerow is an active investor in digital media companies through Lazerow Ventures, an investment fund that has invested in more than 40 technology companies, including Facebook, Tumblr, BuzzFeed, *Mashable,* Domo, Rebel Mouse, and Namely. Visit his personal website at www.lazerow.com.

Luke Owings most recently worked at the Fullbridge Program, overseeing coaching operations. Owings fell in love with the classroom of the twenty-first century when he was fortunate enough to get a job as a teaching fellow while working on his MBA at Harvard Business School in 2011. He plans to continue exploring it globally throughout the current less structured phase of his career on which he recently embarked. Before his time at Harvard Business School, Owings received his BA in economics from Princeton University and spent his early career in McKinsey's Washington, DC, office. Feel free to reach out to Owings at owings.luke@gmail.com.

Michael Radparvar is the cofounder of Holstee, a Brooklyn-based workshop creating products and experiences that help each of us remember what is important. He is the chief storyteller at Holstee, sharing its innovative approach to materials, design, and production with the world. Together with his cofounders, David Radparvar and Fabian Pfortmüller, they have built a values-driven company that has become an iconic brand for its generation. Learn more about Holstee at www.holstee.com.

V. Kasturi Rangan is the Malcolm P. McNair Professor of Marketing at the Harvard Business School and coauthor of *Business Solutions for the Global Poor: Creating Social and Economic Value* and *Transforming Your Go-to-Market Strategy: The Three Disciplines* *of Channel Management.* Until recently the chairman of the marketing department (1998–2002), he is now the cochairman of the school's Social Enterprise Initiative. Visit the Harvard Business School website at www.hbs.edu.

Judith Rodin has served as president of the Rockefeller Foundation since March 2005. A groundbreaking research psychologist, Dr. Rodin was previously the president of the University of Pennsylvania, the first woman to lead an Ivy League institution, and earlier the provost of Yale University. Dr. Rodin is the author of more than 200 academic articles and has written or cowritten 13 books. She has received 19 honorary doctorate degrees and has been named one of Crain's 50 Most Powerful Women in New York. She has also been recognized as one of *Forbes* magazine's World's 100 Most Powerful Women three years in a row. Visit the Rockefeller Foundation website at www.rockfound.org.

ABOUT THE FRANCES HESSELBEIN LEADERSHIP INSTITUTE

We began as the Peter F. Drucker Foundation for Nonprofit Management in 1990 with a simple challenge: How to share the best thinking on leadership and management with our partners in the social, public, and private sectors.

Six weeks after Frances Hesselbein left Girl Scouts of the USA, the largest organization for girls and women in the world, she became the CEO of the smallest foundation in the world, with no money and no staff—just a passionate vision and mission and Board of Governors.

Twenty-five years later, with the contributions of more than 5,000 thought leaders, the organization has published 27 books in 30 languages, and has continually published an Apex Award-winning quarterly Journal, *Leader to Leader*, the essential leadership resource for leaders in business, government, and the social sector. *Leader to Leader* was selected from among

2,075 entries for a 2014 Apex Awards of Excellence in the print category of Magazines, Journals, and Tabloids—Writing. In 2012, the Institute honored founding president Frances Hesselbein by renaming the Institute in her name.

One of the most highly respected experts in the field of contemporary leadership development, Mrs. Hesselbein was awarded the Presidential Medal of Freedom, the United States of America's highest civilian honor, in 1998. The award recognized her leadership as CEO of Girl Scouts of the USA as well as her role as the founding president of this Institute.

By fostering leadership grounded in

- the passion to serve,
- the discipline to listen,
- the courage to question,
- and the spirit to include,

the Hesselbein Institute works to create an open, responsive, global social sector, the equal partner of business and government.

Building on its legacy of innovation, the Hesselbein Institute explores new approaches to strengthen the leadership of the social sector. With sources of talent and inspiration that range from the local community development corporation to the U.S. Army to the corporate boardroom, the Institute helps organizations identify new leaders and new ways of managing that embrace change and abandon the practices of yesterday that no longer achieve results today.

The Hesselbein Institute provides innovative and relevant resources, products, and experiences that enable leaders of the future to address emerging opportunities and challenges. The Institute shares wisdom cultivated over two decades—from its groundbreaking work as the Peter F. Drucker Foundation for Nonprofit Management to its current focus on leadership education and timely management publications—guided by the vision, commitment and spark of Frances Hesselbein.

ACKNOWLEDGMENTS

This book celebrates 25 years of the Frances Hesselbein Leadership Institute—sharing the best thinking on leadership and management with our partners in the social, public and private sectors—and our lasting partnership with John Wiley & Sons. We deeply appreciate all those who helped bring this work to fruition: Peter F. Drucker, Frances Hesselbein, Bernard Banks, Lauren Maillian Bias, Juana Bordas, Adam Braun, Jim Collins, Theresa Drapkin, Caroline Ghosn, Kelly Goldsmith, Marshall Goldsmith, Justine Elyse Green, Nadira Hira, Philip Kotler, Jim Kouzes, Raghu Krishnamoorthy, Kass Lazerow, Mike Lazerow, Luke Owings, Michael Radparvar, V. Kasturi Rangan, and Judith Rodin. Joan Snyder Kuhl championed the vision for this new edition and infused her passion for young leaders throughout its development. We owe the book's focus and structure to our talented writing and publishing colleague, Peter Economy.

We are especially grateful to each member of the Frances Hesselbein Leadership Institute Board of Governors, who enabled this opportunity to become a reality: Chairman Will Conway, Carla Grantham, Joan Snyder Kuhl, Charlie O'Connor and Keith Schaefer. From the bottom of our hearts, we thank you. Your support and guidance will impact lives around the world for years to come. Former Hesselbein Institute Chairman Chris Fralic helped ignite this idea and has been a continual source of guidance and support.

Mutual of America Life Insurance Company and TIAA-CREF are the sole corporate sponsors of this edition of *Peter Drucker's Five Most Important Questions*.

Mutual of America Life Insurance Company was founded in 1945 to serve the financial needs of the nonprofit sector. Mutual of America also recognizes its responsibility as a corporate citizen, to give back to the community it serves. Mutual's sponsorship of this edition is another example of its commitment to serve and support those who dedicate their life's work to caring for those most in need.

Founded in 1918, TIAA-CREF is steadfast in its mission "To serve those who serve others." TIAA-CREF's sponsorship of this book is an acknowledgement of the importance of putting customers first. TIAA-CREF enjoys a rich not-for-profit heritage and is committed to providing a range of solutions to enable lifetime financial well-being for those who are devoted to enriching the lives of others.

To the growing number of Hesselbein "fellow travelers"— Institute supporters, working professionals, community leaders, senior-level executives, cadets, faculty, students, and those who have, and will participate in the Frances Hesselbein Global Academy for Student Leadership and Civic Engagement at the University of Pittsburgh—your energy and passion for leadership is contagious. You are our inspiration, you are the future!